Fit for Business

Matthew Archer

MERCURY BOOKS

Published by W.H. Allen & Co Plc

First published in 1988
by the Mercury Books Division of
W.H. Allen & Co. Plc
44 Hill Street, London W1X 8LB

Set in Palatino by Phoenix Photosetting, Chatham
Printed and bound in Great Britain

British Library Cataloguing in Publication Data

Archer, Matthew
    Fit for business.
    1. Physical fitness   2. Executives——
    Health program
    I. Title
    613.7'088658   RA781

    ISBN 1-85251-045-5

Fit for
Business

TO

BOB GIBSON, JILL BAYLIS, GARY
WARREN, CHRIS WALKER, GARY
TURTON, ADRIAN TURTON, AND ALL
THE OTHER PAST AND PRESENT STAFF
OF CHALFONT LEISURE CENTRE WHO
MAKE SO MANY PEOPLE FIT FOR
BUSINESS.

FOREWORD

THE INCREASING interest being shown by many people in fitness, both physical and mental, is evident from the success of the keep fit classes and health clubs that have blossomed over the last few years. Doctors too have contributed with the identification of the major risk factors for illness, and with their greater ability to screen for them it has been possible to give more definite guidelines for the appropriate 'life-style'.

The method by which this life-style is achieved has to be realistic in terms of the targets set so that life remains enjoyable and fun. Fanaticism often produces eventual disenchantment and ultimately a return to the initial set of problems. Responsibility for the change lies between the individual and his environment, which is increasingly influenced by his occupation. Employers have in this area a great opportunity to provide facilities and the time to foster the necessary changes.

It is unusual to have the subject of the 'healthy life-style' comprehensively discussed from both the business and medical viewpoints and the resulting approach will prove balanced and successful.

Dr S. J. Butcher, MB, BS, MRCGP
General Practitioner and fitness adviser

Contents

INTRODUCTION

THIS BOOK is not written by a doctor, dietitian or famous athlete. My qualification for writing a book about fitness for business executives is simply that I am a business executive and I am fit. In the pages which follow you will find no fancy diets, exhortations to jog 20 miles to work every day or recommendations to drink a daily infusion of stinging nettles!

To become fit and stay that way requires no great agony and there is certainly no necessity to live on a mixture of muesli and grapefruit skins – or whatever other weird diet is recommended by this month's fashionable expert. The busy executive who must travel on business, eat working lunches with customers and attend seminars, receptions and the like, cannot fit the regime and schedule of the ascetic or Olympic athlete into his or her life. In order to stay fit a practical method must be found, one that can be put into practice *as part of* a business life. This book offers a range of alternative ways to do this from which individuals can choose to suit themselves and the nature of their work.

The ideas offered are based on what I hope is a common-sense analysis of what the experts tell us plus my own experience. I have found that an analysis of expert opinion is necessary because, as Alexander Pope said over 250 years ago, 'Who shall decide when doctors disagree?' Every expert, it seems, disagrees with every other in some way, and under those circumstances a choice based on common-sense and personal preference is the only way to come to a conclusion. For example, having read the conflicting views that (a) jogging is good for you and (b) jogging ruins the joints, I found that intensive jogging is so deadly boring that I would rather do something else anyway.

Before launching into the reasons why it is a good idea to be fit for business, I must explain what I mean by 'fit'. Essentially, I mean 'healthy'. However, the pressures of business require the excutive to have physical and mental capabilities above the average so I am recommending 'healthy plus' as your target. This does not mean having an ability to beat Daley Thompson at the next Commonwealth Games but it does mean the ability to perform physical tasks which are reasonably demanding – without the need for three weeks' bed rest and a blood transfusion to get over them. Obviously age and physical make-up will be dominating factors but if you can achieve a good average performance for your age and physique then you may feel much better than you have felt for many years. You will also be likely to be better at your job!

The reader will find that I make recommendations and suggestions to take up activities other than those of the diet and exercise type. There is ample evidence that to be fit for business (e.g. to be able to handle stress) the mind as well as the body needs attention. Whilst there is evidence that exercise can be psychologically beneficial, something else may be needed to help one cope with the mental pressures that can be encountered. The *whole* person needs to be considered and some recommendations are made for 'treatments' which some people may regard as unusual.

I hope that what all this means will becomes clear in the pages which follow.

*Fit for
Business*

PART 1

Why Keep Fit?

1

Fitness and profits

ONE SENSIBLE reason for keeping fit is the probability that the fit person will live longer than the unfit. However, there are lots of other reasons both personal and otherwise and, since the executive should have the support of his or her company in keeping fit, the profit motive is perhaps the best place with which to start.

Hitherto it has been difficult if not impossible to demonstrate that improved fitness in the staff of a company leads to improved profits for the company. Fortunately the evidence is now beginning to emerge.

A number of companies, mostly in North America, having instituted company fitness schemes (e.g. by providing in-house gymnasia), have reported a substantial drop in absenteeism. Canadian Life Assurance Co., for example, reported a 42 per cent (yes, 42 per cent) fall in absenteeism following a fitness programme. This, they estimated, saved them $175,000 a year, which, if gross profits were, say, 10 per cent, would be equivalent to about $1.7 million in sales revenue.

The Prudential Life Assurance Co. produced figures to show that days off per year through sickness for employees *not* on a fitness scheme averaged 8.6. Those on the scheme averaged only 3.5 days per year, with a resulting saving of $285,000 a year. Another American company, Kennecott Copper, cut sickness absence by 55 per cent with a fitness scheme.

There is a remarkable consistency in the results achieved by these companies, which, if their figures are anything to go on, suggests that lost time can be cut by about 50 per cent. However, reduced absenteeism is not the only benefit to be gained. According to the US Institute for Aerobic Research, a study of the performance of a group of salesmen showed markedly increased sales following a fitness programme. The group which followed the programme raised their sales rate by 25 per cent, whilst another group, not following the programme, showed no improvement in performance. The implication is of course that fit people perform better than less fit people – a conclusion which should not be difficult to believe as a result of your own everyday experience and observation.

The British Heart Foundation has also come up with information worthy of some boardroom discussion. They reported, in 1986, that for every 100 male employees on the payroll the average company will lose about 400 days each year through heart disease and circulation problems alone. The Foundation also reported that the UK as a whole loses about 65 *million* man-days a year from heart problems, *plus* another 48 million as a result of coughs and colds and a further 30 million from backache.

The implication in these statistics is obvious. A cash investment in employee health can be a very profitable one. Clearly, the salary cost of absence is not the only loss which occurs when an employee goes sick. Every time someone is absent any of the following can occur:

- Customers are not attended to – possibly resulting in lost orders.

- Disruption to the flow of work – for example, hold-ups in the invoicing department may result in late billing and later payment. In these days when cash flow can be critical no company can afford to delay the despatch of invoices.

- Equipment standing idle – this can range from an unattended machine on the shop floor to a computer at head office.

- Bad decisions, resulting from the absence of someone with important knowledge which would influence a discussion.

The possibilities are many – and expensive

The other side of the story, illustrated by the performances of the two groups of salesmen, is the lost 'production' caused by a generally low level of fitness. The employees may turn up for work but how well do they perform? People with backache, coughs and colds and a general feeling of lassitude tend to drip around all day watching the clock. If companies can find ways to improve the health of their employees, then benefits will accrue in profit terms, resulting from higher productivity and better quality.

What can your company do?

The easiest and cheapest step that a company can take is to insist on *all* employees taking *all* their holidays – including a break of not less than 2 weeks. Executives who believe that the business will collapse if they are away for more than a few days are:

(i)   Deluding themselves,

(ii) Being exploited,

(iii) Working in a very badly managed business, or

(iv) Nut cases who need to see a psychiatrist.

In addition, they are probably heading for a heart attack or nervous breakdown, after which they will be no use to anyone. There are people who actually thrive on a 7-day week made up of 16-hour days, but these are few and far between, and employers should watch the workaholics closely. Failure to do so can result in the loss of a valuable employee, along with his or her know-how, training costs etc.

In addition to 'personnel management' action, companies have a wide choice of measures that they can adopt. These include:

- Provision of a sports field, tennis courts, squash courts, volleyball pitch, bowling alley or some other facility. Multi-gyms with good quality exercise machines are growing in popularity, and although the machinery is expensive, little space is required. The multi-gym gives employees a chance to take some exercise during lunch breaks and after work without the need to organise teams or to lose time travelling.

- Organisation of a sports club or fitness club with competitions, professional coaching and *regular* activities. The annual cricket match between sales and production (or whatever) has virtually no value in fitness terms – something more continuous is needed.

- Arranging health screening with one of the private organisations providing these services. An annual check-up can warn of impending trouble and can head off heart attacks or other medical problems.

- Giving employees a free or subsidised week at a health farm or something more demanding such as an Outward Bound course.

- Making sure that the meals served in company canteens and restaurants are not wholly of the soggy chips variety. Very few workers, even in heavy industry, burn up so many calories that they need a mountain of grease and carbohydrates to see them through the day. A good head cook who knows how to produce nourishing and interesting balanced meals is worth a lot to a company. The burgers and chips specialist could be killing off your staff.

These then are some of the steps that your company can take. Others will become obvious as you read on.

2

Fitness and personal advantage

ONE OF my own reasons for keeping fit is that I enjoy playing games. I was born in 1932, so that my games playing years are running out and I am keen to prolong the pleasure as much as possible. My rugby days are long since gone but I can still enjoy squash, volleyball and basketball. The sheer thrill of winning a good rally or scoring a basket makes all the effort worthwhile, along with the social side, which can provide enjoyable relaxation after a day's work.

Not everyone enjoys playing games, but there are, fortunately, many other advantages which can result from being fit.

Stress and work

It is fashionable these days to talk about stress, a problem which seems to be widely regarded as being peculiar to the twentieth-century senior executive. In fact stress has always been with us and is not limited to senior executives. Indeed, there is some evidence that big bosses are less exposed to stress than their subordinates: a survey carried out by the University of Manchester's Institute of Science and Technology, reported in 1986, showed that miners and policemen have the most stressful jobs, astronomers and librarians have the least stressful and top executives are somewhere in between.

The key factor in deciding whether or not someone is subject to stress is determining what stress really is. There is, I believe, a distinct difference between stress and pressure. The latter comes about from having a lot of work to do and, as my grandmother used to say, 'Hard work never killed anyone'. I think she was right – with the proviso that *overwork* can kill. Overwork can *lead to* stress, which I would define as a physical and mental state brought about by frustration and/or a sense of injustice.

Overwork can cause frustration (the in-tray never seems to empty) and this in turn causes stress. Frustration can also be caused by many other factors, including:

- An indecisive boss

- A stupid or lazy boss

- An unappreciative boss

- An unhelpful boss

- An over-authoritarian boss

We have all experienced one or more of these types, who drive us crazy with their petty rules, unwillingness to listen or understand and total failure to give support to subordinates in difficulty. It is not the big boss who is frustrated, it is the poor bloody infantry who must survive his or her poor style of management.

How does stress show itself?

The symptoms of stress vary from person to person but in each case they are thoroughly unpleasant. The medical experts report the following manifestations:

- Interrupted sleep or insomnia.

- Frequent irritability.

- Lack of, or loss of, a sense of humour.

- Loss of appetite.

- Impaired sex life, e.g. impotence in men.

- Sickness absence, e.g. the regular Monday morning migraine.

- Inefficiency and difficulty in making decisions.

- Increasing dependence on alcohol, cigarettes or drugs.

These are the symptoms; the end result of prolonged stress can be mental illness, heart disease or ulcers.

Fighting stress

One way to fight stress is to change jobs to escape the situation causing the stress. Unfortunately this is not always possible and the chances are the new job will be just as stressful as the old one. Another way is to adopt a positive mental attitude which provides a psychological shield against the daily frustrations and irritations. This is not easy but it can be done, especially if one is fit.

From time to time, like everyone else, I have a really awful day. The trouble usually starts with the railways, which seem to have a permanent plan to kill off their commuter passengers with stress-related diseases. The first two trains will be cancelled and the third packed full with groaning passengers. Having squeezed on, I will stand for 45 minutes (usually in an awkward back-straining posture) while the train stops at all stations and several places in between. Having arrived late at my office, I find that my boss has been looking for me to attend an early meeting no one told me about and which has now started. The meeting drags on while someone with more time than sense bangs on about some trivial point which would be better ignored. Having lost a precious few hours, I am already behind schedule and beginning to worry about the report that I promised would be ready by early afternoon. I hurry through it only to find that my secretary's word processor has broken down . . . and so the day goes on . . . By the time I start the evening battle with the railways (which are keen to prevent me getting home) I am irritable, very tired and feeling distinctly sorry for myself. No doubt you are familiar with this sort of day.

This is the time when we can turn to an instant cure – an hour or so unwinding, followed by a hard work-out. People who are fit find that a good sweat on the squash court, a 20-minute swim or some other form of sustained exercise restores a feeling of well-being and ability to cope. There is, apparently, a well established scientific explanation for this – something to do with burning up the adrenaline which worry, fear or frustration have caused the body to produce. Whatever the medical evidence may be, the fact is that the exercise solution works.

After exercise, a shower and a cold drink you will think more clearly, and all the problems will seem much smaller than before. You may even forgive your boss for his inadequacies – most of them anyway. However, to achieve this 'magical cure' it is necessary to be fit.

The sense of confidence and lack of unused adrenaline which can be achieved by fitness enables one to use the positive mental attitude mentioned above. The technique is simple once the necessary level of confidence is acquired. All that is required is to ask yourself a series of questions and consider the magnitude of the answers. For example:

● Will the problem that is worrying me still be there tomorrow, next week or next month?

In fact, most problems are shortlived and die a natural death. We have only to remember (if we can!) some of last month's worries to realise how many of our working-life agonies are over and done with remarkably quickly.

- What is the worst that can happen?

  The problem will often diminish in terms of worry if an objective view is taken of the worst possible outcome. Many problems are no more than *irritations* or *frustrations* and not really intractable situations at all. Once this is realised, the pressure diminishes or disappears.

- What positive action shall I take?

  Attack may not always be the best form of defence but it is frequently the only effective way to tackle a problem. Many of our working difficulties are caused simply because someone else has taken the initiative and is holding the ring. In such cases there is often no necessity to remain passive. The confident person can take the initiative, hit back and win. There is an added advantage that in hitting back you acquire a reputation for being someone who matters and who cannot be easily pushed around. Once that reputation has been gained, life becomes easier and the problems fewer.

Looking good and feeling good

Healthy people look it. Unhealthy people, in contrast, with pale skin, sagging belly and generally lack-lustre appearance look awful. Look around you on the way to work, in the office or wherever you happen to be. Do you really want to look like old Blenkinsop (he is actually only 45 but looks about 75) or like Mrs Bloggins, whose behind is so vast that it overflows from her chair? No, of course you don't – you want to look no more than your age and to look *capable*. You want to look attractive, not necessarily in a sexual sense, although that can be important too, but in a way which at least means that other people will respect you. If you look good, you will also feel good and both of these benefits come from being fit.

Fit people develop a greater sense of confidence than they would otherwise have and, if you are shy and uncertain of yourself, get going on a fitness campaign and you will find a greater ability to compete. This will show and reflect itself in your work achievements, where a flat stomach and a calm temperament will get you further with customers and colleagues than shyness, bad temper and a beer gut.

Avoiding illnesses

Every winter you will be coughed on, sneezed on and generally bombarded with other people's viruses and bacteria. Resistance to this onslaught is increased by physical fitness, and no amount of mouthwash, gargle or 'tonics' will do you as much good as even a modicum of exercise. Apart from the winter coughs and colds it is apparent from experience and what the experts say, that physical fitness can guard against a whole range of more serious ailments.

The right kind of exercise can cure back pain, repeated headaches and chest pains. This is common experience and it all depends on the cause of the pains. Obviously if your headaches are caused by a tumour on the brain, no amount of jumping up and down in a gymnasium will do any good. If your chest pains are caused by a diseased heart, the same exercise will probably put you out of your misery by bringing about your sudden death. Obviously any unexplained pain is a good reason to visit your doctor for a check-up, but if nothing is found to be wrong, the chances are that your problems are stress-induced and some exercise will do you the world of good.

Let us summarise the ailments which can be guarded against by achieving fitness. They fall into two categories.

(a) *Ailments resulting from a poor diet*. A healthy diet can assist in the prevention of the following:

Constipation
Haemorrhoids
Heart disease
Diabetes
Cancer of the bowel
High blood pressure
Liver disease
Obesity

These diseases are the common ones found in Westernised countries, where the illnesses resulting from underfeeding are virtually non-existent. It is not often that one finds a business executive keeling over with scurvy, and beri-beri is not prevalent in our boardrooms. However, livers ruined by too much alcohol and heart disease encouraged by over-indulgence in animal fats are only too common.

(b) *Ailments made worse by lack of exercise*. Properly planned exercise strengthens muscles, which include the heart. The result will be a reduced chance of heart disease. In addition, exercise has been shown to be beneficial in reducing high blood pressure, which in turn can lead to strokes. Sir David Atkinson, director general of the Chest, Heart and Stroke Association, speaking at the Association's 1986 conference, recommended exercise as one of the way to prevent strokes. At the same conference Dr Anthony Hopkins of St Bartholomew's Hospital, London, reported that 22 per cent of strokes occurred in people under 65 and that strokes were the third commonest cause of death.

Exercise is, in addition, a first-class way to prevent obesity, a condition which can lead to illness.

It seems to be a commonsense conclusion that exercise has a general disease-preventing role. Physical exertion strengthens muscles, exercises joints, expands the lungs, expands the vascular system and generally gets everything going. This surely must do some good. In my own case the only times when I have had periods of being unwell are when for one reason or another I have not been able to indulge in regular exercise. Circumstantial evidence perhaps, but I am not prepared to ignore it.

Enjoying your sex life

A good, enjoyable and active sex life is something that all normal people will want. Having found your ideal partner (perhaps as a result of looking good and feeling good), you will find it frustrating if one of you is too tired, suffering backache or just 'not up to it tonight, darling'.

Good sex requires a reasonable degree of stamina and, if you are that way inclined, some gymnastic ability as well. A fat belly is clearly an impediment and a sudden attack of cramp can be instant death to a passionate hour. The fact is that sexual activity is a form of exercise in itself, so obviously the fitter you are the easier it becomes.

It has been said that top-level athletes have a low sex drive. I doubt that this is true, judging by comments made to me by a friend in Los Angeles who was able to observe the social activity in the Olympic village in 1984. Apparently some international relationships were well established despite the restrictions imposed by training schedules. Some people find physical exercise positively stimulating.

By the way, a newspaper report in 1986 stated that 70 per cent of Frenchmen who are treated for impotence are heavy smokers. The suggestion has been made that smoking causes impotence. It could also be the case that impotence drives men to smoke!

Enjoy a more varied life

If you are unfit, there are lots of things you cannot do – or at least not as well as if you were fit. These activities include:

- All kinds of games.

- Dancing – the modern, energetic kind.

- Playing with your children.

- Strenuous forms of gardening, e.g. heavy digging.

- Demanding forms of DIY, e.g. bricklaying.

- Holiday pursuits such as fell walking.

- Horse riding.

- Cycling.

Even painting a ceiling becomes impossible if you can't wield the brush or roller for 2 minutes without feeling dizzy. The fact is that there are many enjoyable activities, some with a social side, which are difficult to take part in without a reasonable degree of fitness. Sitting in an armchair watching the TV every night is a very narrow and limited way to spend one's spare time and, since we are only allowed three score and ten years, every minute should be used to the full.

Be more efficient at your job

Quite apart from cutting down the sickness absences which will do your promotion prospects no good at all, it pays to be efficient and productive. Our working lives are also more enjoyable if we know that we are efficient and can meet the demands of the job – especially the extra, unexpected demands which turn up just when we thought we could relax a little. Even purely mental work puts a strain on the physical system and such evidence as there is suggests that the physically fit perform mental tasks better for longer. Commonsense suggests that the converse is also true – that an unfit person is likely to perform less effectively.

Business travel, especially by air, can be both physically and mentally exhausting and a fit person will be more able to cope with it. A long trip, say 3 weeks round the major cities of the USA, will include moments of fear (every take-off and landing), plenty of suitcase shifting and goodness knows how many hours standing in queues at airports! All of this can knock the stuffing out of the traveller, who needs to be alert and capable when he or she faces the customer or attends a difficult meeting (at 7.30 am of course). It pays to be fit if one wants to succeed in business. A suitable slogan might be 'Get fit to get on'.

Summary

1. Putting money into employee fitness schemes can be a good investment. Cash savings can be substantial (e.g. in reducing absenteeism) and fit employees will perform better than unfit ones.

2. The individual can benefit in a variety of ways, including:

   - A defence against stress.
   - Looking and feeling good.
   - Avoiding illness.
   - An improved sex life.
   - The chance of a more varied life.
   - Greater personal efficiency at work – and enhanced prospects.

PART 2

Fitness and Exercise

3

The physiological effects of exercise

A COMPREHENSIVE study of the effects of exercise, carried out in the USA from the mid-sixties to 1978, provided evidence in support of the theory that regular exercise prolongs life – providing you don't overdo it.

In the American study, the results of which were reported by Dr R. Paffenbarger of the Stanford University School of Medicine, a total of 17,000 men were monitored. It was found that the men who expended between 2,000 and 3,500 calories per week on exercise had mortality rates between one-quarter and one-third less than those burning fewer calories. This level of calorie consumption works out at about 5 hours of *brisk* walking each week. Alternatively about 4 hours of jogging or 3 hours of squash will produce the same result.

It seems therefore that, if Dr Paffenbarger's studies are anything to go by, the average man (and presumably woman) needs only take a brisk 45-minute walk each day to bring about a significant change. This is good news for those who have neither the time nor the inclination to take prolonged, vigorous exercise, and in the following pages some readily achievable exercise programmes are suggested. It is also a reminder that it is not necessary to put yourself at risk to gain the physical fitness necessary to be a more effective individual in your business life.

Exercise has other beneficial effects in addition to or contributing to those mentioned in Part 1. They include:

1. Increased muscle girth and a reduced proportion of

fatty tissue in the body. The result of this is a better shape and increased agility.

2. More efficient lungs and less laboured breathing.

3. A lowered pulse rate. In other words the heart can do its job with less effort.

4. Reduced blood pressure.

5. Suppression of the appetite – useful if one is trying to lose weight.

These effects allow more work to be done with less effort. However, too much exercise at the wrong time can kill you.

Train, *don't strain*

Jim Fixx, author of books on running and fitness, died at the age of 52 at the end of a 4-mile jogging session. Normally he ran 10 miles a day – every day – and was considered to be a very fit man indeed.

His death has been quoted as an example of 'the dangers of exercise' by those who are, for whatever reason, opposed to it – or perhaps seeking a good excuse not to do it. However, to form a sensible conclusion, it is necessary to look at the circumstances surrounding Fixx's death.

On the day in question, he had driven his car from Cape Cod to the small town of Hardwich in Vermont. This was a 7-hour slog through the weekend traffic *and* in a temperature around the 80 degree mark.

He arrived at his motel fatigued and not having eaten more than a very light breakfast many hours before. The sensible course for Fixx would have been to take a cool shower, relax with a drink and, after a light meal, call it a day. Unfortunately he chose to go for his daily run without any food or rest.

Fixx set off on a circuit which had some sharp inclines and in a rising temperature. Within half a mile he was seen going steadily but already perspiring heavily. Perhaps realising that all was not well, Fixx cut short his run and instead of his normal 10 miles returned to the motel after only 4 miles. He died within 50 yards of the motel.

What then did Fixx do wrong? Firstly, he was fatigued and probably stressed after a long car journey. He gave himself no time to recover from the strain of his journey and, secondly, he had not eaten for many hours. Thirdly, the conditions were bad with a high temperature and a running course with a number of steep inclines. He may also have been dehydrated – a condition which would have worsened rapidly with each minute of perspiration.

It is perhaps ironic that Fixx in his own books warns of the dangers of overdoing it and suggests a sensible attitude to training. His persistence in spite of his own advice is suggestive of the one bad aspect of physical exercise – it is possible to become obsessed with it, psychologically dependent on it and to suffer pangs of guilt if a regular training session is missed.

The rule then should be train, don't strain. Exercise, other than perhaps a gentle walk, should be avoided under the following circumstances:

- When feeling unwell.

- When genuinely fatigued (not just feeling a bit weary).

- When no food has been taken in the last 6–8 hours.

- Within 2½ hours of a heavy meal. According to a report published in *The Lancet*, the workload on the heart can increase by 30 per cent after even a modest meal.

- When thoroughly 'keyed up' – an hour or so to 'unwind' is desirable.

- Within 2½ hours of drinking alcohol.

- Too soon after the last period of strenuous exercise. Dr

Kenneth Cooper, who runs the Dallas Institute for Aerobic Research, recommends a maximum of five exercise sessions a week.

Aches, pains and agonies

Exercise, especially unaccustomed exercise, can cause stiffness, sore muscles and general aches and pains. Some experts have given dire warnings of what these symptoms mean and have been thoroughly discouraging.

For example, the Arthritis and Rheumatism Council has warned that footballers are at risk of developing osteoarthritis in their knee joints. They have also warned of fractures of bones in the joints of soccer, rugby and hockey players.

Sprinters have been warned of tearing muscles, squash players of spraining ankles, tennis players of tennis elbow and golfers of twisted spines. Thankfully, we are told by one expert at least that jogging will not cause osteoarthritis! By contrast, another expert has stated that every step when jogging is equivalent to a *sledgehammer blow* to the joints and thoroughly dangerous.

Does all this mean that exercise will reduce us to a wheelchair existence? I think not, and, to illustrate my point, let me tell you what happened to me.

At the age of 35 I went to the doctor complaining of severe pain in the lower back. The doctor examined me and finding nothing to explain the pain asked me if I had done any heavy lifting. I replied that I had not but had been playing more squash than usual and had been digging the garden. The doctor was horrified and said 'Squash at your age – you must be mad. You will kill yourself'. With additional warnings that I could end up a cripple, the doctor gave me a prescription for some tablets (they turned out to be soluble aspirin) and instructions to limit myself to gentle walks and light gardening.

After a rest of 2 or 3 weeks and the back pain having gone away, I resumed my squash playing. About 15 years later, having added gymnastics, basketball, volleyball and indoor hockey to my leisure activities, I once again had an attack of back pain. This time the pain was really severe and quite debilitating. My doctor referred me to a specialist who, after an examination, solemnly informed me that I needed urgent surgery. Being none too keen on this idea, I asked what the alternative was. The specialist suggested that I could be a cripple for the rest of my life but, after some argument, agreed that physiotherapy *might* work.

After 12 weeks of physiotherapy I was only slightly better and began to wonder if the specialist was right. I decided to have a go at curing myself and, on the principle that if something is regularly moved it won't seize up, I designed my own 'get well' programme. This programme comprised swimming (breast stroke only) and back-strengthening exercises using multi-gym equipment. A daily swim of about 20 minutes each session and a twice weekly half-hour in the multi-gym did the trick and within a month I was back to normal. That was 5 years ago and I am not crippled yet.

Perhaps I was lucky. Perhaps I took a colossal risk. What is certain is that I did not need surgery to recover from my problem and the dire warnings of a wheelchair future have proved groundless. The fact is that I had overdone it and subjected my back to too much strain. I am now much more careful to warm up gently and to resist the temptation to play too much squash too often.

Exercise then can be a cure for aches and pains, including those which were not caused by earlier exercise. Physiotherapy is widely used as a cure for the problems of non-active people and it frequently works. Physiotherapy is in itself a form of exercise. The physiotherapist, by means of manipulation, heat treatment and so on is actually getting bones and muscles to move. Treatments also include carrying out carefully controlled exercises designed to strengthen muscles and loosen up the joints. The same result can be achieved without attending the physiotherapist's clinic by taking up an exercise programme at, say, your local leisure centre.

Once you have developed a reasonable degree of strength and suppleness, continuing the exercises will keep you free of aches and pains – providing you don't overdo it.

4

The psychological effects of exercise

I KNEW a dull, overweight and lack-lustre woman who was obsessed with her physical ailments and thoroughly boring. She wore shabby, dreary clothes and her hair was a greasy mess. Her skin was pale and lifeless and all in all she looked ghastly.

One day she fell in love with a lecturer who was a keen sportsman. Her attempts to attract him were unsuccessful but as part of her campaign she joined an aerobics class which he attended. After a few weeks, and having shed a few pounds, she caught the lecturer's eye. She had, rather to his surprise, developed a more lively personality, which, combined with a more attractive physical appearance, he found rather appealing. Notwithstanding this improvement her love remained unrequited for some months, during which her appearance changed out of all recognition.

Gone was the boring hypochondriac of old – replaced by a confident woman who now wore interesting clothing and had, it seemed, a permanent smile. Eventually she got her man but, after a few months of blissful passion, lost him again. I expected that, under this traumatic blow, she would give up and revert to her old ways. Not a bit of it; she took up regular games playing and added daily jogging to her aerobic work-outs.

I discussed the whole history of this affair with her and this is (roughly) what she told me:

I started aerobics just to be near Tim but after a time I began to feel different. Once I had started losing weight, I found myself going to the classes for reasons other than seeing Tim. I definitely began to feel more confident and I am sure that without the exercise I would not have been able to continue my pursuit of Tim – he ignored me for so long I was tempted to give up hope.

Our brief relationship was sheer heaven and when I lost him, I thought the world had come to an end. It was taking exercise which got me over it and every time I hit rock bottom in my misery I worked even harder. A good work-out always made me feel better and helped me to realise that I am my own person and life is there for living with or without Tim.

The last time I saw her she looked terrific and was totally in control.

So what can exercise do for you psychologically? It can make you feel good, confident and independent. Men can satisfy that macho-ego-need to feel like someone who matters and who can mentally raise two fingers to the world. Women can acquire a sense of confidence similar to that which a touch of make-up gives.

The Health Education Council (now the Health Education Authority) in its booklet 'Looking After Yourself' describes the psychological benefits of exercise in the following ways: 'It helps to control stress', 'It can be great fun', 'It helps you feel good in mind as well as in body'.

Fitness addiction

There is one adverse psychological effect of exercise, the one that was mentioned earlier as probably being at the root of Jim Fixx's death. The adverse effect is that of becoming addicted to exercise and obsessed with the idea that rain or shine the daily 10-mile jog or fifty press-ups is essential.

This obsessive attitude to exercise should be avoided by the simple device of deliberately *not* taking exercise on, say, two days out of every seven and from time to time avoiding it for a whole week. This may not be easy for a small number of people who, apparently, become exercise junkies *physiologically* dependent on exercise. According to some research carried out at London's Guy's Hospital, prolonged exercise causes the body to produce a substance called endorphine which has a chemical similarity to morphine. Not only does endorphine suppress the pains of over-exertion, it is also addictive to certain people.

A spokesman for the British Association of Naturopathy and Osteopathy has been quoted as saying 'I compare fitness addiction with alcoholism. Some people can drink socially and never be affected by alcoholism, while others are hooked after only one drink'.

I have never experienced this form of addiction myself nor have I ever met anyone else who has. However, you may find yourself affected and, if so, check yourself from playing a game or attending a keep-fit session when feeling unwell or fatigued and recognise the psychological trap of feeling that the exercise must be done simply because it is there to be done.

A closer look at stress

First let me remind you of my own idea of what stress is. It is that wound-up feeling caused by frustration. It is that feeling which after a time makes us want to punch someone on the nose or drive too fast after getting out of a traffic jam. It is a condition in which we can become aggressive.

Psychologists tell us that one of the causes of aggression is frustration and there is an explanation for this cause and effect situation. Our stone-age ancestors lived in circumstances of danger and, for example when hunting, conditions which demanded sudden explosive action.

We all know what happens when we are faced with danger or expect to have to act rapidly or violently. Before a 100-metre race an athlete will find himself trembling and his pulse rate will be raised. A pilot taking his plane off the runway experiences the same symptoms and so does an actor about to go on stage for the first time. All these people are experiencing the bodily reactions which equipped our stone-age ancestors for action on which their livelihood or immediate survival depended. Stone-age man *would* react, physically, perhaps by running away or throwing spears. Whatever his physical response was he burned up energy and the adrenaline which causes the pulse rate to rise, the muscles to tense and the respiration rate to increase.

Modern man has no such opportunity to burn off stress when the boss says he is too busy to help with a pressing problem or a train is cancelled yet again. Society forbids us from battering the boss to death or from throwing stones at the station manager. We are left with our adrenaline and our stress and we become bad-tempered and even ill as a result.

Exercise, in the form of a good long walk, a game of badminton or whatever *is* socially permissible, will burn off the adrenaline and restore the individual to a physically *and mentally* normal non-aggressive state. It is not just a form of Eastern oddity that Japanese workers do daily exercises and, in some cases, are provided with punch bags bearing a picture of the boss's face. The psychological value is fairly obvious if after a period of exercise we are relaxed and have lost our aggressive tendencies. Most people think more clearly when calm and relaxed and this is one of the reasons why exercise can make us more effective at work and in greater control of our private lives.

5

The old problem – 'I have no time'

IT HAS been stated that when a man says to the woman he wishes to seduce 'I will love you just as much in the morning as I do now', he is trotting out the world's most overused lie. That may or may not be the case but there is not much doubt that the 'I have no time' excuse for avoiding exercise is the world's most overused piece of self-delusion.

Everyone can find time for exercise – especially if he or she believes it is a necessary part of life in order to be more effective at work, enjoy better health and to live longer. Let's look at some of the possibilities for even the busiest person:

- A daily walk to or from the railway station or to work may well provide a basic 4 or 5 miles a week. If the distance is too great, it may be possible to drive or take the bus part of the way and walk the rest. Yes, this may mean getting up 15 minutes earlier each day – not very enticing in the winter but worth it.

- A lunch-time walk of say ¾ mile each working day will add up to 3¾ miles each week and with a little effort on Saturdays and Sundays can be made up to 5 or 6 miles each week. If the same time is used for jogging, then the amount of exercise taken will be that much increased.

- If there is absolutely no chance of a lunch-time exercise session and walking to and from work is impossible, how about a 15-minute brisk walk each evening before going to bed? This could add up to about 5 miles a week. As one doctor said, 'Buying a dog and taking it for a walk each evening can prevent its owner from suffering heart disease.'

- A 10-minute exercise session can be carried out in the bedroom before retiring. This could be made up of say, 5 minutes on an exercise bicycle (very boring but easier whilst listening to music) followed by 5 minutes of stretching and strength exercises.

- A good look at your weekly programme may well reveal an opportunity for exercise. How much time do you spend watching TV in the evenings? Are there any other totally sedentary periods which could be used? If only *1 hour* a week of this sedentary time is used for walking, jogging, swimming or other gentle exercise, it could make all the difference. Two half-hour sessions may be easier to organise and would probably be more beneficial.

The fact is that if you really want to do so, you can find the time one way or another.

People working for companies enlightened enough to provide exercise facilities for their employees can make full use of them during lunch times and before going home. Even if you are unavoidably working late, why not take an exercise break at normal closing time and then do the extra hours? The exercise will make you feel better and work more efficiently and the change in activity will give your brain a rest. The chances are that you will think more clearly afterwards. There is ample evidence that fatigue reduces efficiency and mental fatigue is no exception. Even a short exercise break will reduce any mental fatigue and provide additional brain power for your late working session.

Some years ago I was working in an Organisation and Methods department and often found myself with a tricky problem to solve and no bright ideas readily forthcoming. I found that more often than not the bright idea would come to me if I left the office and took a brisk walk round the nearby park. We used to say in the department that ordinary problems needed one circuit of the park and really difficult ones needed two circuits. Sometimes the answer to a problem would occur to me (or to one of my colleagues; we all found that the method worked) within the first few minutes, resulting in a dash back to the office to get it down on paper.

Some managers will be aghast at such undisciplined behaviour and insist that their staff could not possibly be allowed to wander off to walk round the park whenever they have a problem to solve. Such managers are stuck in a rut of traditional thinking or simply lacking in imagination. As far as I am concerned, I want answers to problems, and if a walk round the park does the trick, then progress is being made. There is no particular merit in sitting at a desk with an empty mind.

If all else fails, quite a lot of exercise can be gained without formally setting aside any time at all! Even when we yawn and stretch, the body is disposing of carbon dioxide and carrying out muscular work. This principle of taking small doses of exercise can be put to good use. For example:

- Use the stairs, not the lift. If you are so out of condition that walking more than two flights leaves you utterly exhausted, then take the lift for the remainder. After a time you will find you can manage three flights before reaching your limit and so on. Eventually you will not need the lift at all. Walking up (and down) stairs is a good form of exercise which builds up the muscles and gives your heart and lungs something to do.

- Make a habit of 'static exercises'. When standing about, perhaps waiting for a train, raise the heels from the ground and take your weight on your toes. Hold it for a count of seven and lower your heels. This exercise repeated ten times takes just over a minute and strengthens the calf muscles. In addition, almost any body muscles can be exercised by tensing and relaxing them. Pull the tummy into the spine, clench your fists, tense the thigh muscles and so on ten times for each exercise. If you start from your feet and work up, the whole body can be given a work-out, all while waiting for a bus or whatever. In other words if you have no free time at all (which is very unlikely) you can profitably use even 2 minutes while waiting about somewhere.

You can also exercise at your desk both by using static exercises and by standing up from time to time. It has been said that Winston Churchill used a special desk rather like a draughtman's drawing board so that he would work standing up. Standing is better than sitting and it is just as easy, say, to read a report on your own two feet as it is hunched in your chair.

- Do the small chores yourself. Fetching your own coffee requires some movement, as does taking a few photocopies or finding a file in the archives. Asking your secretary to do these jobs gives you no exercise at all.

  Yes, it is taking up valuable time, and yes, you are paid more than your secretary but get the matter in perspective. If you spend an extra 10 minutes a day on your feet to and from the photocopier how does that compare with the time spent in casual chit-chat with colleagues during the day? You don't indulge in casual chit-chat? Give yourself a medal, you are unique!

But all of this, whilst helpful, is no substitute for a good, regular brisk session of exercise which gets the pulse going and the lungs working. People really convinced about the benefits (and the enjoyment) to be gained from exercise will arrange their lives accordingly. The trick is to set aside a period of time each week when *the* priority is the exercise session. Once a regular weekly date has been decided upon, then all the other things to be done can be made to fit round it. Even better is to organise more than one session each week – both to give yourself a better chance of keeping really fit and to provide a fallback position if business travel or other contingencies intervene and force you to miss a session. My own basic programme is made up as follows:

Wednesday evening – keep-fit group session
Friday evening – basketball game
Saturday morning – squash
Sunday evening – squash

There are many weeks when, for one reason or another, I cannot manage all these activities but it is unusual if I cannot keep to two of them. Make up your mind to arrange a good worthwhile exercise session at least once a week. What you do can be chosen to suit your own personal preferences and circumstances.

6

The broad types of exercise

THERE ARE said to be two types of exercise – the so-called aerobic type and the anaerobic. The various forms of exercise within these categories are either of a solitary or a social nature.

Aerobic exercise, as the name implies, is the type which causes the intake of lots of oxygen. In other words, it makes you puff. Squash, steady running and cycling have been placed in this category, whilst swimming, weightlifting and walking have been described as anaerobic. This division is, I think, entirely false and has largely come about as a result of the growth of aerobics classes based on continuous, vigorous movement to music. This activity will certainly cause one to puff if it is done hard enough but so will every other form of exercise. Much depends also on how fit you are. A really fit person may be able to run steadily for, say, 3 minutes before starting to puff, whilst an unfit person will be panting and labouring after 30 seconds.

My own view is that all forms of exercise, whether aerobic or otherwise, have the same effect in the end and it matters little what you do. However, the use of exercise to achieve a better condition is rather like cutting down a tree. You can topple the tree in 15 minutes with a felling axe or in 15 hours using a kitchen knife. In other words, some forms of exercise are more demanding than others and will get you to a chosen level of fitness that much more quickly. The choice of which kind of exercise to go for should take into account not only your personal preferences in terms of enjoyment but also what you can cope with. Remember the slogan – train don't strain. It would be plain silly to try to run a 5-minute mile if you are puffed out after 30 seconds. The disappointment when you are forced to stop will probably be so discouraging that you will give up the idea of exercise altogether – or drop dead if you persist.

My own preferred categorisation, rather than aerobic and anaerobic, is 'stamina exercise' and 'strength exercise'.

Stamina exercises

These are the activities which will give you staying power. They provide the sort of endurance required by hill walkers and infantry. With improved stamina the heart beat is slower and it is possible to keep going longer without shortage of breath.

Stamina exercises develop the circulation and enable the body to obtain more oxygen, more quickly. The best activities for improving stamina are:

Hard swimming	Basketball
Canoeing	Heavy digging
Walking upstairs	Soccer or rugby
Hard cycling	Hill walking
Disco dancing	Jogging
Rowing	Squash

Cricket, ballroom dancing, golf, judo, sailing, yoga, weightlifting and pottering around in the garden will have little or no effect on one's stamina.

Strength exercises

Strength exercises increase the ability to lift and carry heavy weights and generally accomplish work requiring brute force. They also tone up the muscles and can result in a flat tummy and other desirable cosmetic benefits.

The best strength exercises are:

Canoeing	Lawn mowing (with a
Hard cycling	hand mower)
Heavy digging	Rowing
Soccer or rugby	Hard swimming
Gymnastics	Weightlifting

It will be seen that many of the strength exercises are also stamina exercises, so that both results can be achieved from the same activity if required. Most people will probably be content with achieving a fairly modest all-round improvement and will not be too keen on a regime which is particularly demanding. Most people will also look for some fun in their exercise programme and this is more likely to be gained from, say, a friendly game of squash than a dedicated weightlifting lesson. The social aspect can make all the difference to a fitness programme, both in terms of enjoyment and achievement. It all depends on what sort of person you are.

Solitary exercise

There are people who prefer a measure of solitude in their lives and for whom a day's walking in a quiet country area is the nearest thing to paradise. Sometimes normally gregarious people will also need a period of solitude in which to think or just get away from it all. There are a number of activities which can provide the opportunity to be alone, ranging from press-ups and the like in one's own home to jogging for miles or digging the vegetable patch.

Some people find the combination of exercise and solitude

especially therapeutic after a stressful day or a hectic week of meetings, negotiations and travel. Although just sitting alone in a comfortable armchair can be helpful, it can also merely provide the opportunity to brood over troubles and generally make things seem even worse. The benefit of the exercise comes in 'burning off the adrenaline', which makes the thinking process more rational and the world seem a more tolerable place to live in.

Social exercise

In sports such as football, basketball and hockey, team work is required, combined with the likelihood of a get-together in the bar after the game. The joking and leg-pulling which can occur during the après-game period can be extremely therapeutic as a mental relaxation for those whose daily human contact at work is on a deadly serious level. Executives spend most of their day in earnest discussion with their fellows – often, in times of crisis, with little room for superficial chatter or joking. This can make us take life, and ourselves, far too seriously and the team sport provides an antidote. The general banter and teasing which goes on in the changing room after a game can bring us down to earth and encourage one of the best cures for our problems – laughter.

There are of course 'solitary' activities which can be turned into a social activity, e.g. jogging in a group or rambling with a club. One of the great advantages of making these activities into social events is that it makes the work easier. When jogging alone, we are more likely to be conscious of the growing tiredness in our legs than if we are with someone else. It is entirely possible to jog and chat at the same time and by doing so the degree of self-discipline required to keep going is reduced.

Fit for Business

Swimming is another solitary activity which can be socialised. Many would-be swimmers give up simply because they find it boring. Grinding up and down the pool counting the lengths can be very boring indeed and provides little or no mental stimulation. This is a pity, because swimming is a first-class form of exercise. Fortunately it can be made more enjoyable and the following ways can be tried:

- Swim side by side with a partner. It is possible to chat at the same time if the breast stroke is used and swallowing gallons of water is avoided.

- Swim in relays. A group of, say, four people, swimming in two pairs, alternately do a length. This provides a break for one pair whilst the other is swimming.

- Change strokes, e.g. one length breast stroke followed by one length crawl and so on. When combined with relays, the combinations of varied strokes and rest periods break up the monotony.

- Set targets. Either when swimming alone or in a group, setting targets for distance or time or both can act as a stimulus and, once the target is reached, provide a satisfying sense of achievement.

The really important requirement is to obtain enjoyment from your chosen form of exercise. This helps you to keep going and provides much of the psychological benefit.

7

Deciding what to do

THE FIRST and essential requirement is to find out how fit you
are and what you can cope with. If, after many years of
inactivity, you launch out on a determined jog or try to play
squash you are asking for trouble. In such cases you are at
serious risk of damaging a joint or a muscle and, far worse,
you could suffer a cardiac arrest and bring your sporting life
to a sudden end. But don't be afraid, it is only necessary to be
sensible about it. There is of course an outside chance that
you have a heart defect or some other basic problem of which
you are unaware or which you vaguely suspect. Such a
defect could become fatal with even the most cautious
exercise programme, and if you have any doubt at all, go to
your doctor for a general check-up first. Any history of high
blood pressure, chest problems, severe back pain or dizzy
spells is a reason for obtaining qualified medical advice.

Let's suppose that you are in the clear and one of the vast
majority with nothing serious to worry about. The first
thing to do is to give yourself a test.

Testing yourself for stamina

Test A. Walk fairly briskly up and down a flight of stairs
(12–15 steps) three times. If you are puffing too hard to hold
a normal conversation at the end of the test, then you are at

the 'A' stage of fitness (what this means will be explained shortly). If you complete the test without puffing too much, then try the next test, after a rest period of at least 15 minutes.

Test B. Jog steadily on the spot until you are short of breath or feeling tired. Don't force yourself to go on once your breathing is laboured or tiredness becomes uncomfortable. If you can manage 2½ minutes go on to test C. If not, mark yourself down as a B category.

Test C. Jog steadily for ½ mile. If you can do it in 4 minutes or less, regard yourself as category C. If not, you are a B category.

Now, depending on your category, you can choose a fitness training programme. Of course whatever category you are in you can start at the beginning with the As if you prefer and, if you have any doubt, you should do so.

The purpose of the programme which follows is to build you up gradually and gently to a level of fitness where you can safely take up fairly vigorous sports or other strenuous activities. If you are not interested in sports, the later stages of the programme must be carried out regularly to maintain the fitness achieved.

The get fit programme

'A' category start here:

Week 1

Under 50 years	*Over 50 years*
Alternately jog for 15 seconds and walk briskly for 15 seconds for 1 mile.	Walk briskly for 1 mile.

Under 50 years	Over 50 years
or	or
Swim steadily for 15 minutes.	Swim steadily for 10 minutes.

Do this exercise three times a week.

Week 2

Alternately jog for 20 seconds and walk briskly for 10 seconds for 1 mile.	Alternately jog for 10 seconds and walk briskly for 15 seconds for 1 mile.
or	or
Swim steadily for 20 minutes.	Swim steadily for 15 minutes.

Carry out this exercise three times a week.

Week 3

Jog for 30 seconds, walk for 10 seconds for 1 mile.	Jog for 20 seconds, walk for 10 seconds for 1 mile.
or	or
Swim steadily for 25 minutes.	Swim steadily for 20 minutes.

Do this exercise three times a week.

'B' Category start here:

Week 4

Jog for 40 seconds, walk for 10 seconds for 1 mile.	Jog for 30 seconds, walk for 10 seconds for 1 mile.
or	or
Swim steadily for 30 minutes.	Swim steadily for 25 minutes.

Carry out this exercise three times a week.

'C' Category start here:

Week 5

Jog for 60 seconds, walk for 10 seconds for 1 mile.	Jog for 40 seconds, walk for 10 seconds for 1 mile.

Under 50 years	*Over 50 years*
or	*or*
Swim steadily for 30 minutes.	Swim steadily for 25 minutes.

Do this training three times a week.

At the end of week 5 you can now start to step up the effort by either (a) increasing the distance covered or (b) the time in the swimming pool. You can suit yourself, not forgetting the golden rule – train don't strain. If your programme is interrupted, go back to an earlier stage and build up again. If you are feeling really on top of things, speed up the programme by adding distance (jogging) or time (swimming) to suit how you feel. *But* no one will offer you a prize for winning anything so there is no compulsion to overdo it. Likewise, if to make the programme more enjoyable you do it with someone else, do *not* start competing. This can cause one or both of you to overdo it and the 'loser' can be discouraged.

This programme is purely a 'starter'. It may sound rather boring but it can open the doors to a great deal of enjoyment and is well worth the mental and physical discipline required.

Having reached the end of week 5, you should be fit enough to take up some of the less violent sports and/or join a keep-fit club or class. The latter is also a good alternative to the programme suggested, providing you have the confidence to have a go (risking being puffed out before the rest of the class) *and the class is designed for beginners.*

If you are fortunate enough to have a leisure centre nearby with professionals running keep-fit classes, these could be tried as an alternative to the programme, particularly if it is winter time, when jogging can be a bit tough, or if you don't swim.

Your get fit programme can be augmented by other activity if you can find the time. Disco dancing is a good stamina builder and a brisk walk to the station will help.

The next stage

Having, by means of the programme or properly conducted classes, achieved a reasonable level of fitness, why
not start to enjoy your new-found physical abilities by
taking up a sport. There are a number of sports which are
not demanding on beginners. Badminton is a good
example of a fun activity for beginners which does not
become really strenuous until, after considerable practice,
long rallies are achieved.

Other relatively undemanding sports for beginners are:

Table tennis	Judo
Cricket	Sailing
Golf	Tennis
Volleyball	

If you do take up one of these sports, it is important to make
sure that the total exercise completed each week remains
equivalent to week 5 of the programme. A once a week
coaching or practice session on the badminton court will
not amount to much in the way of exercise and you may
have to do additional work in the early stages. It may be
necessary to continue the jogging, swimming or keep-fit
classes until you are playing hard and often and perhaps
even after that. Many sportsmen and women who want to
play well, and prolong their sporting life, indulge in some
other form of exercise as well. Multi-gym (if the facilities are
available) offers a good way to keep yourself fit for hard,
competitive sport, and a weekly swimming session is a
good all round 'improver'.

The 'hard' sports

There are a number of sports which can be tremendously

enjoyable but which should not be attempted until one is really fit. Here are a few to choose from:

Squash

This is a game frequently chosen by overweight executives 'to get fit'. The nature of the game is such that it is necessary to be fit to play it – playing it to get fit is positively dangerous.

The advantages of squash are that the game can be played all the year round and there are many clubs available. To enjoy the game fully the players should be as evenly matched as possible, because only a slight difference in standard will make the game one-sided. Quite a high degree of skill is required to play well, and professional coaching is desirable if the techniques of positioning, tactics and controlling the ball are to be mastered.

Costs vary greatly and some clubs charge absurdly high membership fees, plus court fees. However, most leisure centres provide squash facilities at reasonable prices. A good pair of shoes is a 'must' but beginners need not lash out on an expensive racquet. The cheapest will do until a standard of play is reached at which the more expensive racquet will make a noticeable difference.

Rugby

Most rugby players give up the game by the time they are 30–35 years old, although there are others who go on well past this age and still get a lot of enjoyment. What determines how long to go on with this macho activity depends on a number of factors, including:

- Whether or not the player is enjoying it.

- Whether or not the player can put in enough of the essential training.

- Whether or not the player can still run fast enough to keep up with the scrum or outrun a would-be tackler.

There is another consideration, described by a former top club player like this – 'I finally gave up when the bruises from one Saturday had not healed up in time for the next'.

Soccer

This is another game which most players tend to abandon at an early age. It is also, like rugby, demanding on the legs, heart and lungs but is a game that can be played 'slowly'. By this I mean that if the game is played with others of the same age group, the pace of the game will automatically be adjusted to suit the abilities of the participants. The 20-year-olds in the First XI can go like crazy for every ball and take every opportunity to run the length of the pitch for a chance to score. The 50-year-olds will adopt a more gentlemanly (or, indeed, ladylike) style, often playing a more skilful passing game, with more thought given to tactics and positioning.

Hard cycling

A gentle trip to the shops or even an hour of leisurely pedalling along a country lane does not amount to hard cycling. A 10-mile ride at a speed of 20 miles an hour *is* hard cycling even for a fully fit athlete. For someone less fit a similar journey at half the speed could also be termed hard cycling. Essentially if the cycling fully uses the lungs and heart, the exercise qualifies as one of the 'hard' sports.

One of the features of cycling is its usefulness, as a demanding sport, for people with bad backs, arthritis or problems with the feet. The whole weight of the body is not being carried by the skeleton and there is no jarring of joints or feet. At the same time the heart and lungs are being made to work and many of the muscles are in use. In addition, cycling encourages suppleness and is one of the best exercises for developing staying power.

Hard swimming

Swimming has some of the features of cycling in that there is no jarring of the body and, as a result of the support given by the water, there is little chance of strain. The positive benefits are to be found in the form of stamina *and* strength improvements plus the use of a wide variety of muscles. Swimmers can gain these benefits with little or no risk of damaging a joint or a muscle and, in terms of injuries, the sport is perhaps the safest of all. This makes it particularly suitable for the older executive who would rather not risk the dangers of a collision on the squash court or a pulled muscle on the football pitch.

Long-distance running

Marathons and half-marathons are all the rage these days and clearly show the physical achievements that are possible in 'ordinary' people. Only a few years ago anyone finishing a marathon was regarded as an international hero or heroine and winners were a rare breed. Now many thousands have completed the marathon course, including some who have had little previous running experience and, in a London marathon, a man in his eighties.

Such running is indeed a 'hard' sport, requiring mental strength as well as physical endurance. More practicable in terms of time available and physical abilities is the 4- or 5-mile cross-country run, which, if completed once a week, will maintain a good level of fitness. Depending on age, a 5-mile run should be completed in 30 to 60 minutes to qualify as a hard sport – with allowance being made for weather, gradients and conditions underfoot.

Basketball

Encouraged by television coverage, basketball is a growing sport in the UK, with clubs available fairly widely. The difficulty for the business executive, even if he is a good player, is to find the time required to train to meet the standards set by most clubs.

A way out of this problem is to form your own basketball group, perhaps from colleagues at work or enthusiasts from a keep-fit group. Up to a dozen people will be needed, to play a vigorous game for fun when you are not too bothered about achieving high standards and observing the finer points of the sport.

Full size courts are often hard to find but a smaller court will do if you are prepared to play three or four a side instead of the normal teams of five. An area about one-third normal size is ideal for a modified version of basketball.

Having formed your group and found a suitable court, you play the game under the following simplified rules:

(i)   No penalties are taken. This avoids the need to have a referee, and if the group agree that there will be no *deliberate* body contact, any accidental obstruction of other players can be ignored.

(ii) No 'time-outs' are taken.

(iii) Substitutions are only made if there is an odd number of players and each person takes a turn 'on the bench'.

(iv) The '3 second rule' and the 'keyhole' are ignored.

(v)   No half-time, changing ends, or other stoppages, are observed.

These modifications will be anathema to the purist but for fun players they provide a fast-moving and uninterrupted game. Depending on the size of the court, teams can be of three, four or five players, thus avoiding the difficulty of finding large numbers of participants. When played (nonstop) for 45 minutes, the modified game provides some first-class stamina exercise combined with the use of most muscles.

One advantage of basketball, including the modified version, is that body contact is banned. Unlike rugby or soccer there is only an accidental chance of violent collisions and tackling is not permitted. This makes the game suitable for mixed teams of men and women and also reduces the chance of injury.

Five-a-side football (indoors)

Played with a special soft ball this game is a lot of fun and can be played all year round. Like basketball, the players can modify the rules to suit themselves, including the banning of body contact. Eliminating the barging associated with the outdoor game encourages skill as well as inceasing safety and makes the game more free-flowing.

Players should take it in turns to be goalkeeper, as this position provides little stamina exercise. Some players prefer to have no goalkeeper at all, which can make the game more exciting for defenders, and reduces the numbers required for a good game. If a really fast and exhausting game is wanted, it can be tried with only 3 a side!

8

Exercise and injuries

SOME MEDICAL people seem to be opposed to exercise on the grounds that injury can result from it. One medical writer, for example, had some discouraging words for joggers and jogging. He stated that joggers are not improving their life expectancy by 'pounding along the pavements'. Instead, he warned joggers of such ailments as joint disease and backache and stated that they will probably die sooner than they would otherwise have done. This sounds pretty terrifying as a warning but the word 'probably' appears regularly in such cautionary statements, indicating a degree of uncertainty that there is any positive scientific evidence to support the 'don't do it' lobby. Another warning statement informed us that, when jogging, the joints of the body are 'jiggled round no less than 150 times a minute'. This sounds even more terrifying but isn't that what joints are for? If not, should we spend our lives motionless or perhaps ration our joint jiggles to say 50 a day? How many joint jiggles can we do before it becomes dangerous? The experts do not tell us.

Yet another published warning stated that 'orthopaedic surgeons all over the world report that joggers regularly suffer from problems affecting their hips, spines, shins, feet, knees and ankles'. One might ask which orthopaedic surgeons are reporting these results, and also wonder why, if joggers 'regularly' suffer these problems, they don't simply stop jogging. However, there is even more of this discouragement to think about, including warnings to the effect that jogging can damage the liver, the kidneys and other internal bits and pieces and – horror of horrors! – cause nipple problems. Sportswomen of my acquaintance wear a good quality bra which they tell me eliminates the problem of 'jogger's nipple' – perhaps a visit to Marks and Spencer would provide the remedy for this particular hazard.

Suspiciously unspecific are three other 'don't do it' statements:

- 'It has been *estimated* (my italics) that three out of four joggers injure themselves every year'.

   Who, one may ask, has produced this estimate? One may also wonder at the masochistic tendencies of people who indulge in an activity with an injury probability of 75 per cent, and how many times must they jog each year and for how long in order to suffer this awful result? Clearly the person who covers 5 miles a week is less exposed to injury than the person who covers 50 miles.

- 'It *seems* (my italics) that every year a number of joggers *literally* (my italics) jog themselves into an early grave'. 'It seems' is a bit vague to say the least, as is the expression 'a number of joggers'. What number? Presumably it is somehow known how much longer the deceased joggers would have lived if they had not taken up the exercise. Apart from that, how do we know *for certain* that jogging killed them?

- 'Go into a doctor's office and you'll see would-be athletes queuing up with bad backs . . . and a thousand and one other ailments'. A thousand and one ailments! What does this formidable number include? Presumably cholera, sleeping sickness and chickenpox to make up the number – or are there really that many ailments which are caused by exercise?

The fact is of course that injury *can* result from exercise, as it can result from driving a car, stepping off the pavement or changing a light bulb. It is also a fact that most injury is preventable, and if the following precautions are taken the above dire warnings will have much less relevance.

- Always warm up gently. Before any form of exercise a minute or two of gentle stretching exercise or running on the spot will prepare the body for the more strenuous activity to come. The warm-up will reduce the chance of a pulled muscle.

- Play to the rules. Barging into your opponent on a squash court is not only an infringement of the rules but also positively dangerous, for both of you. Your opponent in any game will expect you to play by the rules, and if you don't, he or she may not be prepared for your aberrant behaviour. This can result in collisions or falls with resulting injury.

- Stay in your peer group. In other words, don't play outside your league. One executive, in his forties, joined in with a group of much younger people who regularly ran round a track as a form of training. Although each person ran at his own pace, the executive tried to keep up with the fittest and fastest. The result was that after four laps of the track he had to give up, vomited and then fainted. Happily, he recovered completely but the result of overdoing it could have been more serious. In short, be sensible, and stay within your limits.

- Wear good shoes. It is not unknown for a beginner to turn up for a keep-fit group wearing £100 worth of designer tracksuit, shorts and so on plus a pair of flashy but useless shoes. Designer kit may be pleasing to the ego but has little other value, and badly designed shoes are a menace. In many sports the feet are made to work hard, and adequate support combined with good cushioning is important. It is important to spend money on quality shoes, whereas any old sweatshirt and tattered shorts will do.

- Obey safety rules. Don't run around the edge of swimming pools, jump in where there are other swimmers – or in any way lark about. If you are a cyclist check your machine regularly to ensure that brakes are working and all the nuts and bolts are present and correct. If you jog, don't run on roads (especially at night), avoid doing too much in hot weather and beware of icy conditions in the winter.

- Stop when something hurts. If a pain develops, regard it as a warning and stop. Pains in the joints can indicate that something is about to give way, and chest pains can indicate something more serious. There will be no medals given for pressing heroically on despite pain, and you may be taking a serious risk. Another warning signal is any feeling of nausea or dizziness, and exercise should be immediately discontinued should these feelings occur.

Taking these precautions can make your sporting activities both safe and enjoyable and, if you are still worried about 'the dangers of jogging', take heart. Dr Terry Gibson of Guy's Hospital has been reported as saying that most sports injuries are 'self-limiting'. According to a report in the *Daily Telegraph* it is Dr Gibson's view that joggers do themselves nothing but good and run no risk of osteo-arthritis.

9

Exercise and age

SOME PEOPLE seem to hold the view that exercise, particularly games playing, is something for young people only. Others seem to think that there is a certain loss of dignity or even something slightly ludicrous about older people playing games. There are those, more often men, who give up participation in sports when their sons beat them on the tennis court or make them look a bit flat-footed at badminton.

All of these are emotional and unreasonable views. Of course, a 20-year-old can run faster than a 50-year-old (normally) and the latter can look a bit silly trying to compete with a younger opponent. But there is no reason why two 50-year-olds cannot enjoy competing with each other. In fact one of the most entertaining sights at a squash club can be the veterans' competition, which, whilst short on rushing around the court, tends to be long on cunning and stroke play.

Until recently one club in the home counties had two regular players both in their late sixties. These two veterans only played each other and it was a sight to behold. Not only did they clearly enjoy themselves immensely but their skill in ball control and positioning always attracted an audience. The fact is that, with careful training and the application of commonsense, age need not be a barrier to sporting activity.

A study reported in the American journal *Primary Care* showed that although physical abilities decreased over the years, the decrease was consistently slower in people continuing with sport and exercise. It was reported that former athletes who remained physically active and did not gain body weight experienced only a modest decrease in ability with the passage of time. Those who became sedentary in life-style and gained weight suffered a decrease in fitness described as 'precipitous'.

The University of Florida's College of Medicine found that cardiovascular changes in active 35- to 55-year-old track runners were less marked than would normally be expected. Similar results were reported in the journal of the American Medical Association, with the conclusion that undesirable alterations in cardiac efficiency, blood chemistry, bone calcium and metabolism can all be delayed through exercise. To add to the evidence, a 10-year study carried out at San Diego University on people with starting ages of 32 to 56 years also showed a distinct slowing down of the ageing process.

So, the first good reason for continuing with exercise as the years go by is the prolongation of physical abilities. There are also living and breathing examples of what older people can achieve. Al Oerter returned to athletics in his late forties and won four gold medals in the Olympic Games between 1956 and 1968 and then went on to reach Olympic trial standard in 1984. Virginia Wade played in leading tennis tournaments at the age of 40 and in sports clubs around the world people of all ages can be seen playing games and enjoying themselves while doing it.

The problem is that people can convince themselves that they are old when they are not. They can feel that it is somehow wrong to move out of the armchair and into the gymnasium simply because they are over 30, over 40, over 50 – or whatever age they consider to be the acceptable limit. There is no biological limit: only a self-inflicted psychological one.

It is also possible to return to exercise and sports after many years of non-active life. Don't believe the people who say that 10 years or more without exercise means that one cannot return to it. Unless a person is suffering from heart disease or some other condition requiring medical attention, a return to exercise is not only possible but also beneficial. Of course the return should be gradual (train, don't strain), including due allowance for any excess weight, underused muscles and heart and lungs which require building up.

Exercise after a heart attack

The Health Education Council have published an interesting booklet entitled 'Beating Heart Disease'. This booklet explains what heart disease is and how it is caused. In addition to recommending exercise as one of the ways to prevent heart attacks, the HEC also makes it clear that exercise is possible *after* an attack.

It is pointed out in the booklet that the heart has a remarkable capacity for healing itself and, although circumstances will vary from one individual to another, a return to exercise is something to aim for. Brisk walking, swimming and cycling are all mentioned in post-heart-attack case studies. The conclusion must be that at any age and even after a heart attack, exercise is possible and beneficial.

Summary

1. Exercise has beneficial physiological effects, including the slowing down of the ageing process and generally improved physical health. However, exercise must be treated with respect if the benefits are to be obtained and it is important to train, not strain.

2. There are beneficial psychological effects to be gained from exercise, including an increase in self-confidence and simply feeling good. Obsession with exercise must be avoided.

3. Stress and its symptoms can be relieved by exercise.

4. The problem of having no time for exercise can be solved. There are ways to include some exercise, however little, in anyone's schedule.

5. Exercise falls broadly into two categories, namely 'stamina exercise' and 'strength exercise'. Some activities provide more of one than the other whilst some provide both.

6. There are forms of exercise suited to people who prefer solitude and those who prefer a more social scene and there are some activities which can be boring. Ways to remove the boredom and enjoy the activity are suggested.

7. There are simple ways to test your fitness, and these, along with a beginners' get-fit programme, are described.

8. Having attained a suitable level of fitness, you can take up various sports – providing enjoyment and a fuller life. These are described within the categories of relatively undemanding sport and 'hard' sports.

9. Exercise can cause injury, but taking some commonsense precautions reduces the risk to acceptable levels.

10. Exercise can be continued into the later years of life and various sports enjoyed long after the conventional 'giving up stage'. A long lay-off is not an insuperable obstacle to taking up exercise – something which can be done even after a heart attack.

PART 3

Eating, Drinking and Fitness

10

What Diet?

THERE IS perhaps more disagreement between the experts on whether or not a particular food or drink is good for you than on any other topic known to man – except religion. The layman who reads the latest reports from some research institute or university which tells him that coffee reduces baldness (or whatever) may be forgiven for being somewhat sceptical. It is likely that only the week before he was told by some other august body that coffee can cause warts on the balls of the feet and that baldness can be halted by eating bone marrow.

The executive concerned about diet (and everyone else) has been bombarded with claims, counterclaims, reports and so-called evidence relating to almost everything edible and drinkable, including:

Fibre, or lack of it	Fish
Fats – saturated and	Vitamins
polyunsaturated	Salt
Sugar	Coffee
Tea	Alcohol

Countless slimming diets have been invented with greater or lesser claims and with as many warnings to avoid them coming from exponents of competitive ideas.

A few years ago potatoes were considered to be death to the waistline and bread was the slimmer's enemy. Now fat and sugar are public enemies 1 and 2, while 'fast food' and synthetic additives appear to be moving rapidly into the target area.

Given all this confusing and contradictory evidence the executive seeking a diet which encourages fitness must rely heavily on a sensible analysis of the evidence. The first dependable conclusion must be that diet *does* influence our health.

We know beyond doubt, for example, that scurvy is caused by a lack of vitamin C and that once the link between scurvy and fresh fruit and vegetables was discovered, the disease was controlled. We also know that rickets, TB and poor physical development were common amongst poor people in the 1920s and 1930s and that these problems disappeared when a better diet was introduced. The school milk programme and the controlled diet of the 1939–1945 war virtually wiped out these 'poverty illnesses'.

There is also ample evidence from the last war of the effects of either not having enough to eat or of having a diet lacking in some essential component. Recent famines in Africa and elsewhere have shown once again the ill effects of inadequate quantity and type of nutrition.

During the 1950s health experts began to express concern that the post-war enthusiasm for sugar, meat and dairy products was creating a new problem. The diet in the Western world, they thought, was likely to lack balance and to be short on vitamins. Concern was expressed that sugar consumption in the UK had reached a new record of 112 lb per head per year. By the 1980s a whole new range of diseases was being linked with the diet of the affluent post-war society with claims that:

- Too much salt can cause strokes and high blood pressure.

- Too much fat can cause high blood pressure.

- Too much sugar causes diabetes and tooth decay.

- Diverticulosis (a problem of the intestine) can be caused by lack of fibre.

- Obesity is caused by too much fat, sugar and non-fibrous carbohydrate.

Whilst there is quite a lot of debate about the validity of these claims (the sugar manufacturers are fighting hard to discredit their opponents), there does seem to be significant evidence that *too much* of something can be as harmful as too little. In short, diet does influence our fitness one way or another.

What then should the business executive do about it? It is not easy, and makes little sense, to chop and change one's diet every time a new report emerges praising or condemning something we eat or drink. Perhaps the first useful step is to clear up some of the myths about foods, leaving the picture a little less confused.

11

Will peanuts improve your sex life?

I SUPPOSE the answer to this question is – 'It all depends on what you do with the peanuts'. There is no evidence that peanuts make any difference one way or another to one's virility or attractiveness – those of us with a sense of adventure could try eating a pound of peanuts a day to see what happens. The peanut/sex life theory is only one of a long list of nonsenses. The following are some of the commoner ones:

- Food grown with the help of natural fertilizer (e.g. horse manure) is more nutritious than food grown with the help of man-made fertilizer.
  Comment: There is no difference in the nutritional value of food grown either way. The confusion has arisen because crop yields vary with the type of fertilizer used.

- Brown eggs are better than white ones.
  Comment: The colour of the shell makes no difference and, in any case, hardly anyone eats the shell.

- An apple a day keeps the doctor away.
  Comment: Other than being a good source of vitamin C, apples are not especially nutritious and have no general curative or preventive properties.

- Honey has life-prolonging properties, will improve the complexion, has aphrodisiac qualities, etc.
  Comment: Honey is a mixture of sugar and water and, apart from its pleasant taste, yields no particular benefits.

- Onions keep away (or cure) colds.
  Comment: No one has yet discovered the cure for the common cold.

- Lettuce and other plants are slimming foods.
  Comment: There is no such thing as a slimming food. It is true that lettuce, cabbage and similar plants contain little in the way of calories and they must be eaten in vast quantities in order to be fattening. However, adding some lettuce to a plate of sausage and chips will not make the meal less fattening.

- Yoghurt prolongs life.
  Comment: There is no proof of this theory except some unconfirmed tales of Russian peasants living to a great age on a diet which *includes* yoghurt. Even if it is true that some of these people live to a great age, yoghurt may not be the reason.

- Spinach builds muscles.
  Comment: Only Popeye has found this to be true. Spinach, like other green vegetables, contains useful vitamins and minerals and more protein than most leaf vegetables but it will not convert an 8-stone weakling into anything else.

- Brown sugar is more nutritious than white.
  Comment: The difference is so slight (about 0.6 milligrams of iron in an ounce of brown sugar) as to be negligible.

- Sea salt is better than ordinary salt.
  Comment: All common salt is sodium chloride (NaCl) wherever it comes from. Sea salt might contain some impurities but it is unlikely that they will be particularly beneficial.

- Fish makes brains.
  Comment: Fish contains vitamin B, which has been claimed to be beneficial to the nervous system. Apart

from that, there is nothing to link fish-eating with intelligence or brain growth.

- Grapefruit (and lemon juice) break up fat.
  Comment: There is no known food which breaks up fat (whatever that means). If a knob of butter is placed on the cut surface of a grapefruit last thing at night, it will still be there in the morning.

- Toast is less fattening than bread.
  Comment: Toast is bread with some of the water driven off. Apart from the colour, there is no other difference.

- Red meat causes gout.
  Comment: The cause of gout is not known.

- Citrus fruits cause rheumatism.
  Comment: The citric acid found in citrus fruits is completely destroyed by the digestive system and does not find its way to the joints to cause pain or anything else.

- Garlic purifies the blood.
  Comment: The kidneys and the liver purify the blood and no amount of garlic makes any difference.

- White wine is less fattening than red.
  Comment: The colour of the wine does not indicate the calories per glass. Sweet wines (of either colour) contain more sugar but the difference is small.

- Carrots improve your eyesight.
  Comment: Vitamin A aids vision in dim light and carrots contain carotin, which the body converts into vitamin A. In the unlikely event that a person in the Western world is deficient in vitamin A, some carrots would help him or her to see better in dim light. *But* no amount of carrots will enable you to throw away your glasses.

- Oysters are an aphrodisiac.

Comment: Oysters probably have the same aphrodisiac powers for Western people as rhinoceros horn has for Orientals. Zero.

These then are some of the myths. There is also the 'grey area' in which competing experts battle it out, leaving the rest of us wondering what is good for us and what is not.

12

When doctors disagree

IT SEEMS that every week someone, somewhere in the world, produces yet another report on diet which either conflicts with previous beliefs or stirs up an unholy row. For the purposes of illustration I have chosen some of the reports produced in only one month, June 1986 – any longer period would be likely to cover so much controversy that it would not fit into this book and would be hopelessly confusing.

June started with a flourish when the comments of Professor Vincent Marks, clinical biochemist at the University of Surrey, were reported in the *Daily Telegraph*. The main points attributed to Professor Marks were:

(i)   He did not think that *any* food was intrinsically bad.

(ii)   Food-faddist parents in the muesli belt of Southern England were effectively starving their children.

(iii)   Food-faddists believed a lot of nutritional nonsense.

(iv)   We are in danger of producing a nation of anorexics.

Professor Marks, it was reported, had annoyed the British Medical Association, which, in its report 'Diet, Nutrition and Health', was putting across the message that there *are* such things as bad foods. The BMA is keen to see a fall in the consumption of sugar, animal fats and salt, and to promote an increase in fibre in the diet.

Professor Marks advocates (sensibly one might think) a

balanced diet containing a little of everything but all in moderation. Perhaps the BMA was influenced by the fact that Professor Marks expressed his views as one of a delegation protesting on behalf of the British Sugar Bureau about the parts of the BMA report which dealt with sugar. However, it is only fair to add that Professor Marks insisted that he was not paid by the Sugar Bureau.

The *Telegraph* also reported the views of Dr John Dawson of the BMA, which include opposition to junk food because it is rich in 'bad things' such as fat and sugar. Professor Marks on the other hand condemns parents who insist on their children eating too many oranges, which, the report says, 'turn your blood yellow'. Gosh!

About a week later another attack on the health food lobby was reported. The *Mail on Sunday* joined the fray with a comment on a book by Professor Arnold Bender, which, said the newspaper, included the view that the health food industry is based on little more than fraud. Professor Bender reported the results of some research carried out in Israel which challenged the widely held view that saturated fats and cholesterol lead to heart disease. It seems that a group of Bedouin eating 'the unhealthiest food imaginable' whilst living in the desert suffered no heart attacks. When these Bedouin were settled in towns on 'an ultra-healthy diet', their blood cholesterol went up and heart disease became common.

Perhaps these unfortunate Arabs had the good luck to read the next edition of the *Sunday Times*, which, on 15 June, reported that aspirin had been found to reduce the chance of coronaries. Admittedly, Dr Clifford Barger of the Harvard Medical School, who did the research, suggests that a diet low in animal fat should be *combined* with aspirin. Apparently a hormone called prostaglandin affects the arteries so that they become narrower and more likely to be blocked. The blockage increases the chance of a heart attack. Aspirin, we are told, counteracts the prostaglandin.

In addition, Dr Barger is reported as saying that the prostaglandins are produced by fat (I always thought that hormones were produced by various glands in the body, but never mind) and therefore fat is bad for us. Dr Barger also pointed to the fact that people in poor countries who eat little animal fat have fewer heart attacks. It could be of course that many of them die of hunger or diseases of malnutrition before they have a chance to suffer a heart attack.

The end of June saw a revival of the great sugar controversy described in an article in the *Daily Telegraph* by Caroline Walker, the nutritionist and writer. Apparently Ms Walker had previously written an article about food trade organisations and the quality of the information they supply to the press on the subject of food and health. Not unreasonably she had proposed that information from industry sources should not be treated as impartial. A response from a Professor Durnin (who had spoken previously on behalf of the Sugar Bureau) claimed that there is 'virtually (sic) no connection between sugar intake and obesity'.

Professor Durnin, we are told, went on to claim that there is very little relation between reducing the amount of sugar in the diet and the successful treatment of obesity. 'These scientific facts,' Professor Durnin is reported as saying, 'when they appeared – usually very unobtrusively – in some medical journals . . . infuriated the nutritional missionaries . . .'

Ms Walker also came under attack from Professor Yudkin, who had previously spoken on behalf of the Butter Information Council. This is not surprising, as Ms Walker had warned about the dangers of fat – the main constituent of butter.

All of this was reported in just one month. In the course of a year the layman is at the receiving end of much more conflicting opinion and just does not know who to believe. Incidentally, the obsession with sugar cropped up again in October 1986 with the publication of a report by the US Food and Drug Administration which was reported as saying that 'There is no conclusive evidence that demonstrates a hazard to the general public when sugars are consumed at the levels that are now current'.

Not surprisingly the sugar industry was delighted with this statement – no doubt it was more than a little worried that over recent years about fifty national and international committees had recommended cutting down on sugar consumption. The *Independent* reported the chairman of the Sugar Bureau as describing the FDA report as 'marvellous news for the food industry'. The chairman went on to say that almost 1,000 scientific papers had been reviewed, with the conclusion that 'sugar is not responsible for diseases such as obesity, diabetes, hyperactivity, hypertension or cancer'.

However, Professor Hegsted of Harvard University is reported as arguing that 'The facts in the report are right but the interpretation is unfortunate. The question that has not been asked is what are the advantages and what are the disadvantages of a diet high in sugar. There are no advantages, but there are disadvantages . . .' So the squabble went on, with contributions on sugar and obesity, sugar and gallstones and sugar and kidney stones from a Bristol University professor and similar anti-sugar comments from the Center for Science in the Public Interest in Washington DC.

It is perhaps not surprising that in cases where a lot of bitter dispute has taken place a commercial interest can be seen. The sugar industry is not the only one to fight against attacks on its product. In recent times advertising on behalf of bread manufacturers, butter suppliers and milk producers has been orientated towards the claimed health-giving properties of their products. Butter manufacturers, for example, have been at pains to point out that margarine contains as much fat as butter, although carefully omitting any reference to differences in *type* of fat.

Fortunately for the consumer there are areas of general agreement or where the evidence produced by disinterested investigators is fairly convincing. Let's take a look at what seem to be the more reliable conclusions.

13

Some more reliable conclusions

Fibre

There is significant evidence to suggest that a lack of fibre in the diet can give rise to various disorders of the bowel, including diverticulitis (a serious form of inflammation) and piles. Some investigations have suggested that heart disease is encouraged by a lack of fibre, and the practical daily experience of most people is that a diet lacking fibre causes constipation or, at least, irregularity in bowel movements. There is also evidence from poorer and less developed societies living on a high fibre diet that these ailments are much less prevalent in those countries. The conclusion must be therefore that fibre should form a sub-stantial part of an executive's diet, and it can be obtained from:

- Wholemeal bread – fibre content around 9 per cent as opposed to white bread which contains about 3 per cent fibre.

- High-fibre breakfast cereals.

- Porridge.

- Pulses, e.g. beans, peas and lentils.

- Fruit and vegetables.

Fats

The link between *too much* fat and heart disease is fairly well established – well enough to take note of it. All forms of fat are packed with calories, so if you are also concerned about your waistline, cutting down will at least help to prevent your bulges getting worse. The main sources of fat are:

- Butter and margarine.
- Cakes, pastries and biscuits.
- Full cream milk and cream.
- Meat.
- Cheese.
- Fried food.
- Chocolate.

There are variations in fat content between the items on this list which can be exploited to satisfy personal preferences and to keep the diet interesting. The fat content of cheese, for instance, varies widely from one type to another. Cottage cheese contains only about 4 per cent fat, whilst at the other end of the scale cream cheese is almost half fat. Edam and Camembert have about 23 per cent fat and most processed cheese about 25 per cent. There is therefore a fairly wide range of the less fatty alternatives for the cheese fanatics to choose from. Meat also varies in fat content, with chicken one of the least fatty. Fish can also be substituted for meat, with a saving in calories. Skimmed milk contains only 0.1 per cent fat as against full cream milk, which varies from 3.8 per cent to 4.8 per cent. Using skimmed milk provides much the same amount of calcium and protein as the other milks, so there is no loss of these nutrients.

Sugar

The average person in the UK is said to consume about 85 lb of sugar per year. Imagine eighty-five 1 lb bags of sugar in a pile and you get some idea of what is being consumed.

The main argument against sugar is that it provides calories *but nothing else*. A diet containing a lot of sugar (e.g. cakes, soft drinks, puddings) is likely to provide ample energy but possibly not enough protein and fibre.

There is a theory that some people become addicted to sugar (the so-called sweet tooth) and if such people consume the average of 85 lb a year, that will provide enough energy to walk about 2,000 miles! Since very few business people walk that far in a year, the result is a bigger waistline as all the surplus will be converted to fat. Perhaps Grannie's warning that eating sweets between meals will 'spoil your lunch' was based on a lot of good sense. If the appetite for other food is reduced by eating too much sugar, then the diet can become unbalanced.

One of the simplest ways to cut down on sugar is to stop taking it in tea and coffee. I used to take sugar in tea and realised that, with a fairly high tea consumption, I was consuming about 24 teaspoonfuls of sugar a day. I weighed out 24 teaspoonfuls and found that it added up to 6 oz. This worked out to 137 lb a year! Combined with an unknown additional quantity that I was consuming in biscuits, cakes, puddings and the like, I felt that this was excessive to say the least. I promptly gave up sugar in tea (and also on cereals) and although, at first, I found the tea rather unpalatable, after about 2 weeks I became adjusted to it. I now find that sugar in tea is quite disgusting. My dentist was delighted and, without knowing that I had reduced my sugar intake, commented, on my next check-up, that my teeth and gums showed an improvement. She asked if I had changed my diet!

Protein

An essential part of the diet, protein is adequately provided by any balanced diet. Fears that cutting down on meat will result in a shortage of protein are unfounded. The Health Education Council states that on average we eat twice as much protein as we need and that any surplus to requirements makes no difference.

Protein is available in fish, pulses, bread, potatoes, milk, eggs and much else, so cutting down on your meat consumption (to reduce fat intake) will cause no problem, providing enough of the other foods are taken instead.

Salt

There is some evidence to support the theory that too much salt can lead to high blood pressure. Unfortunately food manufacturers add salt to a wide range of products, which makes the job of avoiding it that much more difficult. However, some manufactured food products are now sold as being low in salt or having no added salt and these can be chosen if preferred. Otherwise, salt can be reduced or omitted when cooking and there is no compulsion to sprinkle additional salt on food before eating it. Various 'nibbles' such as crisps and nuts are often salted, and these too can be avoided.

These are some of the main opinions about food which seem to be reasonabie and well supported. In summary, the recommendations for a diet that will contribute to fitness will include the following:

(i)   Include fibre in the diet.

(ii)   Reduce fat intake.

(iii)   Reduce sugar intake.

(iv)   Reduce salt intake.

Following this advice should not be too difficult even if a lot of business lunches and dinners are an unavoidable part of life. It seems that a varied diet – eating whatever is preferred but keeping to the four recommendations above – will produce the desired result.

14

Are there any other dire warnings?

UNFORTUNATELY, YES. Regular reports appear pointing out the dangers of eating something or not eating it. Some of the pronouncements are clearly the obsessions of cranks or even a promotion of something which someone wishes to sell. It is interesting to talk to employees of shops such as Boots, who will tell you that the morning after a TV programme in which someone extols the virtues of a mineral, a vitamin, castor oil or whatever, there is a mad rush of customers for the product. Examples reported by an employee of a large retail chemist include:

- Cod liver oil – as a remedy for arthritis.

- Zinc compounds – to 'cure spots' and for prevention of anorexia nervosa.

- A mixture of Epsom salt, sodium bicarbonate and Glauber salt – as a cure for rheumatism.

- Evening primrose oil – as a cure for pre-menstrual tension.

- Ginseng – to improve sexual performance.

- Garlic pearls – to aid digestion, 'cure' catarrh and 'purify the blood'.

There seems to be little solid evidence that any of these items will do what the customers thought they would do, although there have been some research results that suggest a link between zinc deficiency and some forms of mental illness. There was also a claim from a consultant pharmacologist, reported in the *British Medical Journal* in October 1986, that garlic can stop the blood clots which cause heart attacks. The claim was also made that garlic kills germs. However, it was explained that the garlic must be *eaten raw* because cooking destroys the active agents, methyl allyl trisulphide and diallyl disulphide, which respectively prevent the clots and kill the bugs.

Cholesterol

A fatty substance, much in the news in recent years, is believed by many authorities to encourage atherosclerosis and coronary heart disease. Atherosclerosis is a condition in which the inner walls of blood vessels become thickened and distorted by an accumulation of fatty deposits, fibrous tissue and blood clots. The accumulation of these deposits can significantly reduce the diameter of the blood vessels, with the result that blood supply to related tissues can be cut off. This can cause the tissues to die as a result of oxygen starvation, and should the heart be affected, the result can be fatal. It makes sense therefore to assume that the warnings about cholesterol encouraging atherosclerosis are correct and to take steps to minimise the amount of cholesterol in the diet.

There is some evidence that merely being overweight encourages atherosclerosis – perhaps because surplus body fat is related to an excess of fat (and cholesterol) in the bloodstream. However, the following foods contain high levels of cholesterol and should perhaps be avoided or cut down:

Milk (except skimmed milk)
Butter
Dripping
Sausages

Cream
Lard
Bacon
Cakes, biscuits, puddings and pastry

These are all foods containing *saturated* fats, which provide most of the cholesterol. Some less fatty foods also include quite a lot of cholesterol and these include:

Veal
Liver
Egg (yolk only)

Brains
Kidney

Foods containing *unsaturated* fats which can be substituted for some of the above items are vegetable oils, soft margarine and fish.

In practice, especially if being entertained by someone else, it is not so easy to pick and choose and, in particular, to choose meals low in saturated fats or other sources of cholesterol. The best and simplest approach seems to be to simply cut down on fat all round. When eating out, the following tips will help:

- Take smaller helpings of anything fatty.

- Avoid putting butter on your bread.

- Cut all the visible fat off your meat.

- Order grilled food, not fried.

- Avoid rich sauces, e.g. the cream and brandy variety.

- Choose fresh fruit salad rather than cheesecake for a sweet.

Much the same 'rules' can be applied at home where you can make use of vegetable oils rather than animal fats for cooking. By following these rules a significant reduction in fat intake can be achieved and, say, by substituting fish for meat, the saturated fats can be avoided.

It has been shown that exercise has a beneficial effect in reducing the incidence of atherosclerosis and that a regular work-out reduces the level of blood cholesterol. There is, conversely, evidence that heavy smoking and excessive alcohol consumption can contribute to the development of atherosclerosis but whether or not there is any link between smoking, alcohol and cholesterol is not clear.

Calcium

In recent years much attention has been paid to a disease called osteoporosis, which affects women in particular. Osteoporosis is a wasting away of the bone, resulting, in the late fifties and the sixties, in brittle bones and a humped back. Men are far less prone to this condition as it is linked to hormonal changes occurring after the menopause.

Osteoporosis, therefore, is essentially a disease of ageing, but it can be speeded up by diabetes, arthritis, an over-active thyroid – and malnutrition. The symptoms are not limited to a rounded back and brittle bones but may also include back pains (resulting from weakened vertebrae becoming compressed), indigestion and breathing difficulties.

The condition is irreversible and there is no evidence that a diet high in calcium is a preventative. Calcium is important for proper nerve and muscle functions, controlling blood cholesterol and stimulating the flow of milk when breast-feeding. Best sources of calcium are:

Skimmed milk	Wholemeal bread
Cheese	Yoghurt
Vegetables	Canned fish
Nuts	Tap water, in hard water areas

Calcium intake illustrates how important a balanced diet is, since it has been shown that a high fibre diet can easily be lacking in calcium, and phytic acid (found in raw vegetables and cereals) can prevent calcium absorption. There is always the possibility therefore that someone who 'goes overboard' on a 'health food' diet can end up with calcium deficiency!

Other suggested influences on calcium absorption include an excess of phosphates (found in processed foods and soft drinks) and too little protein. Both of these are alleged to reduce calcium absorption, and so is a diet *very high* in protein!

Once again exercise can be helpful and Dr Morris Notelovitz of the University of Florida College of Medicine recommends an exercise session two or three times a week. Dr Notelovitz believes that exercise can stimulate new bone formation, especially up to the age of 35 years. After 35, bone is lost as part of the ageing process but exercise, says Notelovitz, will slow down the rate of loss.

Other influences on calcium deficiency are coffee and alcohol consumption. Both of these beverages, taken in excess, are said to encourage calcium deficiency.

Coffee

The average cup of coffee contains about 3 per cent caffeine, which after a 38-year study, some American investigators have concluded encourages heart disease. Among the findings of the famous Johns Hopkins Medical Institution in Baltimore are that:

● Even one or two cups of coffee a day appear to be associated with an extra risk of heart disease.

- People drinking more than five cups a day are three times as likely to suffer heart disease as those who drink none at all.

- Coffee drinkers are more at risk of suffering angina, heart attacks and coronaries than non-drinkers.

- Older people are likely to be more sensitive to coffee than younger people.

It is only fair to say that other studies have found no links between coffee drinking and heart problems but it has been pointed out that coffee drinkers are often also smokers. It is the smoking that has been blamed for the heart problems rather than the coffee. Studies reported in 1986 appear to separate the coffee risks from the smoking risks, exposing coffee as a danger.

Caffeine is a stimulant which, it is said, can upset the regularity of the heart beat and may also encourage an increase in blood cholesterol. Incidentally, caffeine is also present in tea and certain cola drinks.

Perhaps needless to say, the coffee manufacturers have not been silent on the subject, and a spokesman for Nestlé was reported in the press (*Independent*, October 1986) as saying 'There have been more than 10,000 reports . . . about coffee and none have come up with any evidence that moderate consumption of coffee does the average person any harm'. The choice of the words 'moderate consumption' and 'average person' should be noted.

15

The terrifying conclusions so far

READERS MUST by now have formed the conclusion that just about every food and drink is potentially or actually lethal. The wonder is that anyone survives adolescence, let alone lives long enough to collect a pension. We are told that fat, sugar, salt, coffee and more besides can kill. We all know that smoking is dangerous and we could be having guilt feelings about that comforting gin and tonic – or even a refreshing soft drink gratefully consumed on a hot summer day.

What then is the commonsense answer? Clearly, since the human race survives and we all know of a gluttonous, heavy drinking, chain smoker who lived to a ripe old age, there are no absolutes and there is an optimum life-style for everyone. This optimum life-style should include avoidance of excess in any one direction *and* allow some indulgence in the pleasures of life such as the odd drink, a good cigar and a tasty meal. A certain amount of indulgence is necessary to be able to relax, and a convivial evening centred on a good dinner can be a useful contribution to reducing stress and reviving the flagging spirits.

There are two extremes to be avoided if fitness is to be achieved, and I suggest the following 'types' as representing these extremes.

The Hedonist

- Drives a car – everywhere, even 100 yards to buy another carton of fags. Never walks if it can possibly be avoided.

- Has no time for exercise, not even a game of golf. Work, sitting at a desk, is paramount.

- Is significantly overweight – the bulging waistline and sagging bottom are hidden away by carefully tailored clothing.

- Starts the day with a big, greasy breakfast – the egg, bacon, sausage and thickly-buttered toast are believed to be essential to cope with the day.

- Lunch – either a pint and a pie pub lunch, eaten in a hurry while leaning on a crowded bar, *or* a 3-hour, four-course event accompanied by aperitifs, wine and brandy.

- Evening meal – either a business dinner much the same as lunch, a convenience food meal or a cholesterol packed mountain – 'which everyone needs after a hard day'.

- Holidays – if taken at all, 2 weeks in a hotel with a daily stroll (25 yards) to the poolside to spend the day on a lounger. Plenty of cooling drinks (alcohol-based) are consumed plus of course three hearty meals a day. A cruise with much the same ingredients may be preferred.

The Ascetic

- Cycles or runs everywhere – however tired, he regards the use of the internal combustion engine as 'wasteful' and damaging to the environment.

- Exercises obsessively – a 10-mile jog every day, rain or shine and even when feeling unwell.

- Is all skin and bone – regards the least trace of body fat as disgusting and spends much time in front of the mirror looking for it.

- Breakfast – a glass of sugar-reduced orange or carrot juice.

- Lunch – one piece of celery, half a grapefruit and a bowl of muesli.

- Evening meal – a bowl of fat-reduced, sugar-free, salt-substitute soup and an orange.

- Holidays – 2 weeks hill-walking. The evenings are spent at youth hostels or camp sites looking for smokers and drinkers to berate.

In between these two extremes is the person, who, wishing to be physically and mentally fit, finds a relaxed but controlled way to live. This person I suggest will:

- Take regular exercise suited to age and preference but will not overdo it.

- Will eat balanced meals, including 'a little of what you fancy'.

- Will consume modest amounts of alcohol, normally as an adjunct to a meal.

- Will take relaxing holidays which are neither an exercise in overeating or an extended version of SAS survival training.

I will not provide a list of strict rules such as 'Thou shalt not eat white bread' or 'Thou shalt not drink strong liquors' as readers will be quite capable of working out their own idea of what they wish to do or not do. I make no apology, however, for the general rules suggested above, as they seem to me to be commonsense and take due note of the views of most of the experts.

16

Fatness, fitness and dieting

IN ADDITION to considering our diet as an influence on
fitness we should also take a look at dieting. This is a subject
which seem to be permanently with us and kept alive by
organisations such as Weight Watchers and a considerable
number of magazines devoted to the subject. Even in
magazines covering a wide range of general subjects,
articles on dieting are commonly found. Each January, for
example, there is a rash of articles with such titles as 'Shape
up for the New Year', 'Trim your figure for the holidays'
and 'Two special diets for the New Year'.

There is, in addition, a whole industry of manufacturers
making a living from people intent on dieting. Findus, the
food manufacturers, offer their 'Lean Cuisine' dishes;
Cambridge Nutrition Ltd sell specially prepared food
under the name 'The Cambridge Diet'; and Heinz offer
'weight watchers' jams containing less sugar than ordinary
jam. Nor does the dieting industry stop there. Slimming
pills are advertised and there are even self-hypnosis tape
recordings to assist in achieving weight loss.

Clearly an awful lot of people attach a great deal of
importance to losing weight. What then are the benefits all
these slimmers are trying to gain? The most obvious benefit
being sought is the cosmetic one. Western culture, as
demonstrated in beauty competitions, fashion magazines
and the media in general, regards a slim figure as one of the
constituents of the 'beautiful person'. This applies,
although perhaps not equally, to men as well as women.
However, most of the advertising is aimed at women, with

subtle and not so subtle play on increasing physical attractiveness to men. 'My husband says it's like being married to a new woman' is the slogan at the top of an advertisement for an organisation offering weekly slimming classes. Another advertisement, less obvious in its message, features a young and beautiful girl who is alleged to use the herbal product being promoted. In an article on slimming, a successful slimmer (size 14 down to size 10) is shown in a glamorous gown nonchalantly leaning on an exercise machine that is being used by a hunky man in T-shirt (bulging biceps of course) and track suit trousers.

All this emphasis on being beautiful – and by implication being attractive to the opposite sex – can distract attention from the following two important questions:

- How important is it for business people to avoid being overweight?

- Is dieting essential or even beneficial?

The first question has already been mentioned in earlier pages but a few more comments are needed.

Financial benefits of avoiding overweight

There is just one financial benefit which might be gained and that is in a reduction of your life insurance premium. Insurance company statistics suggest that for every 10 per cent over a person's 'recommended weight' (discussed later in this section) the death rate increases by 13 per cent. For this reason virtually all companies charge higher premiums for people they consider to be overweight and lower premiums for the slim. However, not all insurance underwriters are blessed with a great intellect and it is possible to obtain a policy when weighing an acceptable 10 stone and still be insured at the same premium after 10 years of gluttony have increased the weight to 20 stone!

Fitness and being overweight

If the statistics tell us that fat people die younger, then it is clearly healthier not to be overweight – unless you have survived to about 60, after which the danger is less. Death is, after all, the ultimate in being unfit.

There is ample evidence to show that seriously over-weight people are prone to a range of diseases, including high blood pressure and gall bladder ailments. It has also been suggested that arthritis is encouraged by being overweight.

In addition to the results of medical and other scientific research, there is ample anecdotal evidence to link levels of fitness with varying levels of weight for any individual. A frequent comment from people who have lost weight is how much fitter they feel. This may of course have a psychological basis, since the feeling of achievement in shedding a few pounds should in itself produce a sense of well-being. However, athletes lose performance when overweight and regain it when the weight is lost. Even just one or two pounds can make a difference, which all suggests that there is an optimum weight for looking good, feeling good and being fit.

Is dieting essential or even beneficial?

The primary purpose of dieting is to lose weight and, on the face of it, this seems a reasonable enough objective. If body weight depends on the balance between calories absorbed in food eaten and energy output, then reducing the former should result in weight loss if energy output remains constant or increases. This, the scientifically minded will recognise, fits in with the first law of thermodynamics, which states that in a system of constant mass, energy can be neither created nor destroyed.

Why is it then that some people go on a diet and yet complain that they do not become any slimmer? There are a number of theories to explain this phenomenon.

The starvation theory

Dieting is really another name for planned starvation. The starvation theory says that when our food intake falls, our metabolic rate falls with it. This, it is said, is a natural protective mechanism which, by making our bodies use food more efficiently, slows down the loss of fat and other tissues. In other words, the body automatically compensates for a shortage of food and minimises the effect of the dieting.

The fat protection theory

A recently published notion is that in our polluted and filthy world fat is used to store, and render harmless, various toxic substances that are taken into our bodies. The theory has it that toxins absorbed from tobacco smoke, diesel fumes, impure drinking water, processed foods and other sources are deposited in the fatty tissues. If by dieting we try to use up the fatty tissues, the body will resist to prevent the toxins entering the bloodstream. The result is once again a slowing down of the metabolic rate *plus*, at an advanced stage, the use by the body of valuable lean tissue to produce energy. In this way, muscle tissue, including the heart, is burned up, with resulting potentially serious consequences. At best the dieter will remain flabby, since the fat will still be there whilst the supporting tissue will be reduced.

This theory is also used to explain the occurrence of heart attacks amongst dieters and also amongst novice joggers. It has been claimed by Dr Arabella Melville and Colin Johnson in their book *Persistent Fat and How to Lose It* that over-enthusiastic joggers can 'release poisoned fat' into their bodies and 'poison the struggling heart'.

The cheat theory

There are undoubtedly some people who cheat on their diets and some who are unaware of the cheating. One unsuccessful dieter was observed to eat (between carefully planned meals) two slices of fruit cake, one banana, one 4 oz chocolate bar and several biscuits. All this extra food was consumed in one day. The person concerned complained 'I have been on this diet for two weeks and I have lost no weight at all'.

The dieting makes you fat theory

An extension to the starvation theory, this one argues that having slowed down the metabolic rate by dieting, the body gains even more weight than before when a normal diet is resumed. In other words, the dieter ends up with a more fuel-efficient body and gets fatter still when the diet is discontinued.

There is, then, quite a large question mark over dieting both as a means to permanently lose weight and to improve fitness. In addition, there are a number of crank diets which have been introduced over the years which appear to be positively dangerous. Among those which have come (and gone) are:

- The grapefruit diet, in which all meals comprised half a grapefruit to start with and bacon and egg to follow.

- The banana diet, consisting entirely of – yes, bananas.

Neither of these diets appear to provide a proper balance of fat, protein and carbohydrate and they possibly lack vitamins and minerals as well. No doubt they work, since, apart from being unbelievably boring, they are a form of malnutrition. No doubt anyone eating a restricted diet consisting entirely of carrots or onions or smoked salmon would also lose weight – and after a time end up in hospital seriously ill.

A number of other diets, some with catchy titles such as 'The Drinking Man's Diet' purport to allow the dieter to eat whatever he or she likes. These sound very appealing but in fact such diets eliminate carbohydrates. One effect of restricting carbohydrates is to lose body water, thus resulting in a loss of weight. The resulting dehydration can cause nasty side-effects, including severe fatigue and faintness.

These 'wonder diets' are in fact playing tricks with the body, and whilst sometimes bringing about the desired weight loss, are also putting the dieter at risk. All dieting which depends on restricting food intake to one or two items is likely to be dangerous, and any diet which says 'you can eat as much as you like' is probably a confidence trick.

Will slimming pills help?

From time to time someone comes up with a 'slimming pill'. These are often highly compressed 'bulking agents', which, when swallowed, absorb water and swell. The result is that the stomach feels full and the appetite is suppressed. This mechanical method will probably work with most people to some degree as long as they don't mind risking constipation. Incidentally, a high fibre food such as All-Bran will have a similar 'filling up' effect at half the price, twice the pleasure and be nutritious as well.

Which? magazine reported in September 1983 on a slimming pill and concluded that the particular product concerned could provide some psychological support during a diet but nothing more.

Pills containing drugs should be avoided like the plague unless prescribed by a competent and qualified medical practitioner. Drugs which are said to suppress the appetite exist, but they can have unpleasant side-effects and once started may become a necessity.

Other aspects of dieting

Reducing our food intake requires discipline. It is this need for discipline which can be the downfall of many would-be slimmers, and anything which makes it harder should be avoided. Some of the proprietary diets such as all-liquid foods are unutterably boring (even if providing balanced nutrition) and expensive. Equally boring are the endless salads (no dressing of course) recommended with monotonous regularity and, if one is travelling on business, difficult to adhere to. The average railway buffet car or airline menu does not provide the foods to meet the tougher regimes and it is next to impossible to persuade the steward to mix up a patent liquid diet.

It is also difficult if entertaining or being entertained to nibble away at a stick of celery while your guest or host wishes to tuck into steak and French fries plus three other courses. Any insistence on keeping to a serious diet on these occasions can embarrass your companion and will not enhance your business prospects. It is important therefore to find a way to reduce weight (if required) or prevent weight gain in a way which is practicable and socially acceptable.

The executive's diet

The diet for the executive who wishes to lose weight is exactly the same as the one chosen to keep fit – only less of it. If a decision has been made to cut down on fats and sugar for fitness reasons, it is likely that the number of calories will be reduced as well. This gets the slimming process started but, if not enough, a reduction of food all round will do the trick. Yes, this requires discipline too, but not nearly as much as if one of the special diets were chosen.

It simply means eating one less British Rail sandwich (that should not be too difficult) or leaving the plastic cheese on the airline's plastic tray. Other tips include those already recommended for reducing fat such as choosing grilled rather than fried food plus the following:

- Skip the starter if you can. If you can't, go for melon, grapefruit, smoked salmon or something similar. Fried whitebait, prawn cocktail and anything else containing fat should be avoided.

- Choose a fish dish rather than meat and stop the waiter from loading too many potatoes on your plate.

- Avoid eating your bread roll or, at least, eat it without butter.

- Choose *fresh* fruit salad for dessert but if you really enjoy puddings and the like, leave a third of it on your plate. Of course if you can skip dessert altogether so much the better if you are trying to reduce weight.

- After the meal try to get some exercise such as a brief but brisk walk. Although 20 minutes walking will only use up about 100 calories (equal perhaps to your unbuttered roll), it all helps.

One executive who successfully lost weight simply halved his portions (including when eating out) but continued to eat everything he liked. Once down to the weight he wanted, he ate about two-thirds of his previous quantities. He found this tough at first but after only 3 to 4 days on the half portion regime he became adjusted, and keeping to a maximum of two-thirds at the later stage was easy.

Vegetarian diets

There has long been a lobby for vegetarian diets both as a means of weight control and as a means of becoming fitter. Some research carried out in Australia in 1986 produced what is probably the first proof that there are benefits from vegetarianism, at least as far as fitness is concerned.

A number of people were placed on a vegetarian diet (which included milk and eggs) for 6 weeks. The diet avoided meat and fish of all kinds but included wholegrain cereals, wholemeal bread and *double* the amount of fruit and vegetables that the subjects normally ate. The result was a significant drop in blood pressure but no change in body weight. The conclusion was that the vegetarian content of the diet improved the health of the subjects despite the fact that their consumption of salt was not changed and they smoked and drank alcohol as usual.

Other researchers, this time in Munich, also concluded that vegetarians could be healthier. The results of some studies on about 100 people and reported at the end of 1986 in the *British Journal of Nutrition*, indicated that vegetarians have less viscous blood. In everyday terms this means that vegetarians have thinner blood and, it was suggested, would be less prone to heart disease. Thicker blood it seems is more likely to clot and block the arteries.

Based on this evidence it is not unreasonable to suppose that a vegetarian diet will improve fitness, and if taken in reduced quantities, will result in weight loss as well.

What weight should you be?

According to charts published by the Health Education Council a man 5ft 8in. tall should weigh between 126 lb and 154 lb. A woman of the same height should weigh exactly the same.

According to the Royal College of Physicians a man 5ft 8in. tall should weigh between 132 lb and 166 lb. A woman of the same height should weigh between 122 lb and 154 lb.

A booklet entitled '7 day diet plan' produced by Boots Plc differentiates between small, medium and large frame people and recommends, for medium-frame people 5ft 8in. tall, a weight of 149 lb (men) and 144 lb (women).

It will be seen that there is some variation in the expert views.

In my own case, when 5ft 8in. tall at the age of 18, I weighed 156 lb, which is outside the range permitted by the HEC but acceptable to the Royal College of Physicians. Since I regard myself as a 'medium frame', I was also about half a stone heavier than Boots would recommend. The fact is that at the time I was in my school rugby and athletics teams, swam regularly, boxed and had regular training sessions in the gym and on the track. I was as fit as a fiddle and had not the slightest appearance of being fat.

The implication is that the much referred to height and weight tables can at best be only a very general guide and a more down to earth indication is necessary. Since we all have variations in body structure and even the tables permit some variation, perhaps the best test is a visual one.

One easy test is to stand naked in front of a full-length mirror and jump up and down. If anything wobbles which shouldn't wobble, that is fat. Alternatively stand up straight and squeeze the flesh at the hips and abdomen. Can you grab a handful? If yes, that's fat too.

This type of test seems to me to be more sensible than referring to a table of theoretical figures. Not only does the obvious surplus fat show what is there to be removed for the purposes of cosmetic improvement, but also shows the surplus weight being carried around. The surplus weight will be a strain on the body and an impediment to physical activity. It should also be borne in mind that *some* fat is probably essential to good health. A body composed of skin and bone and little else has no reserves to cope with illness or a temporary period of starvation. Recent expert comment has it that *some* increase in weight as the years go by is normal and desirable.

17

Vitamins

THERE IS, without any doubt, a connection between vitamins and fitness. Shortage of any vitamin results in illness, and some prolonged shortages in death. Whilst this is the stark truth, most of the people taking vitamin pills are wasting their money and, since the body excretes surpluses, are merely adding vitamins to the nation's sewage.

Only minute quantities of vitamins are required to maintain good health and a varied diet will provide them. In fact, it is possible to overdose on vitamins A and D, which are poisonous in large quantities. There is another danger in taking vitamin supplement tablets in that many of them contain iron, which, if taken in excess, can cause damage to the lining of the stomach.

Which? magazine in a January 1984 report on vitamins referred to a survey carried out in 1981 which showed that about 1 in 1,000 hospital casualty patients had overdosed on vitamin pills.

Vitamins belong to one or other of two types – watersoluble and fat-soluble. The water-soluble vitamins are B and C, and although they are normally present in all body cells, are not stored in large quantities. The fat-soluble vitamins (A, D, E and K) are stored in the liver, and there is normally enough present to last the average person for several months. It is the water-soluble vitamins which need to be topped up on a regular basis but it is these vitamins which are excreted when any surplus is taken on board.

Vitamin D is interesting in that most of what is needed is

made in the skin in response to sunlight. A shortage of vitamin D could result from covering oneself in clothing from head to foot combined with a diet lacking in the vitamin. It was a lack of vitamin D which caused the rickets so common in the children of poor families in industrial countries in earlier days. Many lived in the industrial cities under a permanent pall of smoke and dust which effectively screened out the sun's rays. The resulting lack of vitamin D prevented calcium being absorbed from the diet, which in turn resulted in soft bones and the classic symptoms of bandy legs, fractures and stunted growth associated with rickets. However, this type of deficiency is now rare in Western countries, easily corrected and unlikely to manifest itself in the boardrooms of industry.

False claims about vitamins

In addition to the honest but unproven theory already mentioned, that vitamin C can be helpful in dealing with the common cold, there have also been some nut-case ideas put forward. There have also been some quite disgracefully false or misleading claims made simply to sell a product or to sell a book. It is a fact that if someone comes up with a 'magical formula' for fitness, sexual potency, weight control, preventing baldness or whatever, then thousands of innocent people will want to know the details. If the details are provided in a well publicised book, it will sell like crazy and make the author very rich.

Vitamins have been used in the past to provide the so-called magic formulae which include:

- Niacin, a B type vitamin, to prevent the 'Monday morning feeling'. In other words, if you stuff yourself with vitamin B, you will become a super go-go person who never dreads the start of another week.

- Inosital, another B type, to cure baldness.

- Vitamin E to *cure* muscular dystrophy. This claim is especially disgusting as it can raise false hopes in the sufferers of this terrible disease.

One promoter of these ideas, now dead, made a good living from books, TV appearances, radio talks and magazine articles.

The trick used in promoting these ideas as a commercial venture is to take some sound nutritional advice and mix it with some wild speculation for which there is no evidence whatsoever. The sound advice provides an appearance of respectability which causes the victim to believe the doubtful part.

The facts about vitamins can be obtained from responsible bodies such as the Health Education Authority, Royal College of Physicians and the various research institutions. As long ago as 1966 the Food Standards Committee recommended that the following claims for vitamins should not be made:

- That vitamin supplements are needed when taking a full, mixed diet.

- That more than 400 units of vitamin D are needed each day.

- That nervousness and/or lack of energy are *only* due to lack of vitamins.

- That normally healthy people can be made to look younger by taking extra vitamins.

One advertisement for a food supplement product stated that it was specially formulated for a nutritionist, now over 70 years old, who, it is claimed, 'has never been ill and has more energy than men half his age'. This may be true but is not necessarily true for anyone else and may not result from taking the advertised product.

The advertisement also drew attention to poor nutrition

as 'the *hidden* (my italics) menace to health and vitality' and went on to refer to people who consider themselves well fed as being 'among its victims'. Cleverly, the advertisement referred to 'a thoughtless, unbalanced diet . . .' which could mean that . . . 'vital nutrients are in short supply'.

Cleverly, because the advertisement, by implication at least, was not saying that a good, balanced diet will be short of vital nutrients but rather that even if you think you are well fed, you could still be among the 'victims'.

The product concerned was not just a mere collection of vitamins. The contents were stated to include a whole range of minerals (including sodium which is a constituent of common salt) plus a lengthy list of 'Extra Nutrients'. These extra nutrients included:

P-aminobenzoic acid	Glutamic acid
Choline bitartrate	L-cysteine
Inositol	monohydrochloride
Betaine hydrochloride	Bioflavonoid complex
Rutin	D L-methronine

plus (naturally) kelp and alfalfa

What these substances are supposed to do one can only guess. One can only guess what they *are* for that matter, although most of us know that kelp is a kind of seaweed and alfalfa is a leguminous plant of the pea family.

Another vitamin supplement product is advertised as containing additional extras. Among the constituents of this formula are:

Potassium (as orotate)
Hesperidin
Apricot kernels
Horsetail grass
Golden seal root

and, of course, kelp and alfalfa.

It seems that the manufacturers vie with each other to produce longer and longer additions to the vitamins and, by including such things as apricot kernels, imply that they are essential to a healthy life. 'Scientific' names and terms are also used despite the fact that the average person has no idea what they mean. Have you any idea what hesperidin is, or potassium *as orotate*? No? Well don't feel inadequate, the *Penguin Dictionary of Science* doesn't either.

Another incomprehensible statement in an advertisement is 'Co-factors in Bio-Synthesis of GLA and Prostgland in E . . .' (Presumably the advertisers made a mistake and meant to say Prostaglandin E.) What this means is probably only clear to a trained biochemist but the advertisement does give some help. The next few words are '. . . vital to Women's Physiology'. Terrific, now all the women who were worried that they were lacking the co-factor in Bio-Synthesis of their GLA and Prostgland in E can do something about it.

People can make up their own minds as to whether or not they are convinced by these advertisements but should bear in mind that the great burden of the evidence is that supplementary vitamins (with or without Hesperidin and Horsetail grass) are unnecessary if a normal but balanced diet is taken.

Cooking and vitamins

Cooking can destroy vitamins but it is unlikely to reduce their content to a dangerously low level. Some vitamins will be dissolved into the cooking water, so if this water is used for sauces, they will not be lost. However, it is not a bad idea to eat as much raw food as possible or at least to cook it lightly in order to get the most out of it.

Vegetables stored before cooking will lose some vitamin

content owing to the effect of sunlight, so it helps to keep them in the dark. Milk is also affected by sunlight and the vitamin content will be preserved by keeping the bottle covered – or buying milk in cartons.

When choosing fruit and vegetables, avoid the old and wilting items. The fresher the food, the higher the vitamin content.

Alcohol, smoking and vitamins

There is evidence that both alcohol and smoking destroy vitamins in the body. Vitamin C, for example, is said to be destroyed by cigarette smoking but, since the incidence of scurvy amongst smokers seems to be limited and the pubs are not full of people with rickets, any danger of vitamin C deficiency seems slight. Naturally, the manufacturers of vitamin pills will encourage magazine articles and the like which mention this subject.

18

Additives

MUCH PUBLICITY has been given to the use of additives in food and there has been much argument about this practice. Food manufacturers argue that the additives are beneficial to consumers in various ways, whilst opponents of additives argue the reverse.

Manufacturers will say, for example, that preservatives prolong the safe life of food in the distribution chain and reduce the chance of a consumer suffering from eating something which has gone off. This is probably true but it is also true that prolonging the life of the food is very convenient for manufacturers, wholesalers and retailers. Not only will wastage costs be reduced but the distribution system *need not be so finely tuned*. Manufacturers will argue that it is more cost-effective to be able to store and transport products in bulk and not to have to worry about meeting a close deadline. This also means that systems for control of distribution can be relatively inefficient and more tolerant of delays and foul-ups.

The decision that the consumer has to make is whether he or she would prefer the food with or without the preservatives (and other additives). The natural food lobby argues that although only approved additives are used, no one knows what their full effect may be – including any cumulative effects. There has been some evidence to link certain additives with hyperactivity in children and, by implication, psychological problems and allergies in adults.

Once again intelligent individuals can make up their own minds and, insofar as supplies allow, choose food which does not contain additives if they prefer. What though, apart from preservatives, are we considering? The following are commonly used additives:

Colourings   Lubricants
Artificial flavouring   Binders
Sweeteners   Coatings
Fillers   Anti-oxidants

These substances can vary in chemical content and, it has been reasonably argued, if precisely the same substance is found in nature, it should not be offensive to the natural food lobby. There is no doubt that a chemical made in a test tube is no different from the same chemical found in, say, cabbage leaves, and the fact that it is 'synthetic' or man-made is irrelevant. What is relevant though is the quantity present in natural foods as opposed to processed foods. Because sodium chloride (common salt) may be present in minute traces in freshly dug vegetables, it does not mean that it is OK to shove relatively huge quantities into tinned soup.

However, a report issued by the Food Policy Research Unit in 1986 stated that fears about food additives were exaggerated. The author of the report, Dr V. Wheelock of Bradford University, said, according to the press, that the public was being brainwashed into believing that natural food was safe.

Similarly, at a debate of the British Association for the Advancement of Science in September 1986, Dr Peter King, head of the Society of the Chemical Industry, accused opponents of additives of being 'do gooders in the social conscience industry'. Dr King argued that chlorine is added to drinking water without calls for the practice to be discontinued. Perhaps not, but at the same debate Dr Erik Millstone of Sussex University's science policy research unit is said to have criticised the secrecy of food regulating bodies. Dr Millstone argued that official safety reassurances were not scientifically based and that of the 4,000 or so additives used in food scientists were absolutely sure about the safety of only a dozen.

So, once again the doctors disagree and it might be prudent to err on the side of caution and avoid as many of the 4,000 additives as possible by eating freshly prepared food whenever possible.

19

The demon drink

ALCOHOL IS a subject worthy of special mention as it forms a significant part of both the private and business lives of so many people. Indeed, for many one of the great pleasures of life is a glass of a good wine taken with a well prepared meal or a gin and tonic gratefully consumed at the end of a difficult day. The occasional drink can be beneficial as well as enjoyable in that it can help us to unwind and can counteract stress. Alcoholics are of course a different category and suffer the misfortune that the smallest quantity of alcohol can lead to disastrous results.

Regardless of any benefits of alcohol there are, let's face it, disadvantages and dangers and the business person is as vulnerable to them as anyone else. Let's take a look at the bad news.

Alcohol and dieting

All forms of alcoholic drinks contain calories. A pint of beer will add around 180 calories to the daily intake and even a so-called low-calorie drink is unlikely to be worth less than 100 calories.

Clearly this must be taken into account when dieting – along with the warning that cutting down on food and replacing it with alcohol can be dangerous. The calorie count may remain the same but malnutrition can result from what has become an unbalanced diet.

Alcohol and performance

Both physical and mental performance are impaired by alcohol – even small quantities of alcohol. This is a demonstrable fact, as is also the fact that, having consumed alcohol, many people sincerely believe that their performance has not deteriorated or even that it has improved.

In a test carried out with a group of professional drivers the more they drank, the more certain they were that they were able to negotiate a test course. But when put to the test, it was shown that the more they drank, the *less* they were able to do it. This has implications not only for sales representatives and others who drive as part of their jobs but everyone else as well.

The effect of alcohol on a typist is likely to include a larger than normal number of errors and the effects on a machine operator on the shop floor can include a nasty accident.

A leading campaigner against alcoholism was reported, in October 1986, as saying that one in ten people have their judgement and ability to function properly at work impaired by alcohol. At a conference of personnel managers it was claimed that many businessmen and managing directors are among the main culprits – and would fail a Breathalyser test if it was given to them after lunch.

Whilst it is difficult to assess the number of business executives who are seriously affected by alcohol, it is clear that too much booze impairs judgement. In pre-Gorbachev days a businessman negotiating a deal with the Russians was subject to hard bargaining and a lot of vodka. The vodka was no accident. The Russian negotiators were only too well aware that a favourable deal can more easily be made with someone whose mental faculties are dulled by booze.

Nor it is an accident that some of the major financial organisations in the City of London ban spirits in their diningrooms and boardrooms. No one who is slowed down by alcohol is 'fit for business'.

The effect of a few drinks can not only be quite severe in many cases but also long-lasting. It takes the body about one hour to clear the alcohol from the bloodstream for each 'unit' of drink consumed. A unit, or standard drink, is provided by half a pint of beer, so someone who has consumed 4 pints needs 8 hours to return to normal. It is not difficult therefore to enjoy a convivial business lunch and to be below normal 'operating level' for the rest of the working day.

One senior executive of my acquaintance was *hors de combat* for the whole of almost every afternoon and was found on some occasions sound asleep at his desk. He was too senior to be sacked but his juniors and colleagues much resented the problems that his behaviour gave them.

Alcohol and disease

According to the Health Education Authority, the long-term effects of heavy drinking can include the following conditions:

Hepatitis of the liver
Cirrhosis of the liver
Stomach disorders
Cancer of the mouth,
    throat and gullet
Brain damage

Sexual difficulties
Psychiatric disorders
High blood pressure
Muscle disease
Vitamin deficiency

On top of all this lot there is the common or garden hangover, which, whilst not likely to be fatal, can put the sufferer out of action for a day.

One question to be answered is 'What constitutes heavy drinking?'

According to the HEC, men should limit themselves to twenty standard drinks per week and women to thirteen. Consumption above this level is pushing your luck, especially if most of the drinking is concentrated into two or three sessions. Anything over fifty standard drinks per week for men and thirty-five for women is positively dangerous and will almost certainly affect your health as well as your ability to work.

The reason why women should consume less than men is that the water content of a woman's body is lower than that of a man. About 60 per cent of the body weight of men is made up of water whilst in women it is about 50 per cent. Since alcohol is distributed through the body fluids, it is more 'diluted' in men than women. In addition, a woman's liver is more prone to damage from alcohol than that of a man.

The action needed to be 'fit for business'

It is not always easy for, say, a salesman to keep his drinking within reasonable limits when every third customer turns out to be an enthusiastic tippler. Nor is it easy, without causing offence, to refuse a drink in certain circumstances. Perhaps because of the drink/driving publicity of recent years, most people are generally more sensible and understanding than in the past but difficult situations can still be encountered.

Companies can do their bit by eliminating spirits from the drinks available at in-house receptions, lunches etc., and generally discouraging lengthy pre- and post-lunch sessions. One major international company bans *all* alcohol on its premises.

Individuals can try one or more of the following methods:

- Sticking to tonic water or tomato juice. If it matters what other people think, one can always pretend it is gin or a Bloody Mary.

- Spin out the drinks – easier if a long drink is chosen.

- Plead a stomach ailment and ask for fruit juice.

- Say you are driving and hope the other people are smart enough not to press you.

I had the problem solved for me when, after years of moderate drinking, I found that alcohol of any kind was making me ill. Apparently some form of allergy had developed and I have found that everyone readily accepts this reason for refusal. Most people I meet are remarkably sympathetic – as they should be!

The commercial cost

Estimates of the cost to industry of alcohol abuse run as high as £1,350,000,000 per year in the UK alone. This estimate was given to a 1986 conference by Douglas Allsop of the Scottish Council of Alcohol and by Karen Howard, managing director of the consultants, Howard Affiliates.

These costs, it was claimed, arise from sickness absence and premature death brought about through alcohol abuse. There must be other hidden costs to add to the £1.35 billion, such as the cost of errors made, sales lost, recruitment of replacement staff and so on. The total cost could be as high as £2.0 billion – equivalent to about £20 billion in gross sales revenue!

Alcohol and additives

Earlier in this section comment was made on the use of additives in food. According to the Campaign for Real Ale (CAMRA), many beers contain additives too. CAMRA have listed arsenic, cadmium, lead and zinc as common additives. Not surprisingly, the brewers have hit back and the chairman of one major brewing company described CAMRA's complaint as an 'irresponsible onslaught . . . full of dangerous generalisation'. A Brewers' Society spokesman has been reported as saying that the chemicals cited by CAMRA are not used in brewing and that if they were in the beer, they would have come from natural raw materials. This spokesman also stated that they would be present in microscopically low quantities.

To add fuel to the flames, it was reported in the *Daily Mail* in October 1986 that five kegs of British beer were destroyed by the German authorities, who found it was unfit for human consumption under their rules. The reason? Additives. It seems that among the collection of substances used in brewing are fish-gut extract, onion skins, flaked maize, potatoes, Epsom salts and, as one agent for British beers put it, 'dyes more suited to kippers or day-glo T-shirts'.

CHEERS!

Summary

1. There is much disagreement amongst experts as to what constitutes a healthy diet. The picture is further complicated by some well established myths, such as brown eggs being better than white ones.

2. From the conflicting evidence (described) it is possible to pick out some commonsense conclusions. There are also some dangers to watch out for, such as too much cholesterol in the diet or lack of calcium.

3. Analysis suggests that to be fit for business is best achieved by taking a middle course – avoiding excess on the one hand or asceticism on the other. Cutting down on fats, sugar and salt appear to be good general rules, as does including fibre in the diet.

4. Dieting both to look better and be more healthy is discussed and the evidence seems to be that specific diets are a waste of time or even dangerous. A modest reduction all round whilst keeping to a varied and balanced diet should do the trick if you are overweight as a result of overeating.

5. Vitamin supplements are generally unnecessary and a waste of money and misleading claims about vitamins should be recognised as such and ignored.

6. A sensible approach to additives is needed and intelligent people can make up their own minds as to whether they avoid them by eating freshly prepared foods.

7. Alcohol, which can be beneficial in moderate quantities, can be

extremely damaging to the individual and costly to industry when abused. Limits to weekly consumption and ways to achieve the right level are suggested.

PART 4

Overworked, Underpaid and Fed up

20

Tired and anxious

FROM TIME to time we are all fed up with our jobs, sometimes bored and sometimes overworked. Obviously these
are situations we will wish to avoid, because, whether we
like it or not, we have to spend 8 or more hours a day at our
jobs. There is no joy in being miserable for 8 hours a day (or,
in the worst cases, all our waking hours), so it makes sense
to look for ways to solve the problem. Apart from that,
continuous periods of dissatisfaction or unhappiness
reduce mental and physical fitness, which in turn creates
more misery and generates a vicious spiral, downwards. In
this part we shall look at a number of defence mechanisms
and escape routes that can help to keep us fit for business.

In Part 1 we looked at stress, a potentially serious state
often caused by the frustrations which people face in their
business lives. Much more common is a *sub-stress* state,
which, whilst less likely to result in heart failure or a mental
breakdown, acts as a drag on performance and efficiency.
The problem was well illustrated by the results of a study
carried out in 1986 by *Chief Executive* magazine.

In the study 233 managing directors, mostly in their forties
and fifties, were questioned. The startling results were:

- Nearly two-thirds considered that their sexual activities were
  diminished as a result of a heavy workload.

- One-third were too tired to go out with friends.

- Nearly two-thirds said work pressure made them irritable and
  43 per cent were short-tempered towards colleagues.

The average working week for the group was 53 hours and only 5 per cent worked less than 40 hours a week. More than a quarter of these managing directors put in more than 60 hours a week. Perhaps surprisingly, two-thirds of the people questioned were actually seeking *more* work and responsibility, despite the fact that many of them had been told by their doctors to ease up.

Here is a good example of the sub-stress situation. Despite irritability and being short-tempered with colleagues (a situation which does *not* encourage a good corporate performance) and a clearly damaged domestic and social life, most of these workaholics were looking for even more pressure. No doubt ambition has a lot to do with it but, as Bertrand Russell put it, 'One of the symptoms of an approaching nervous breakdown is the belief that one's work is terribly important'.

One workaholic boss included in his many functions the job of teaching trainees for executive jobs. He held daily 'surgeries' individually with each trainee – with disastrous results. The boss would greet the trainee with a grunt, wave him to a chair and open the folder containing the work to be reviewed. After a few minutes of smouldering silence a dialogue such as this would take place:

Boss (sarcastically): Are you aware or are you not that customs regulations in Outer Mongolia forbid the import of dried egg?

Trainee (trembling): Oh, er, er, yes sir.

Boss (even more sarcastically): Oh, you *are* aware. Are you also aware that freight rates are calculated from the port of loading?

Trainee (now terrified): I think so, sir.

Boss (exploding): Then why the hell do you bring me this bloody rubbish containing two serious errors, etc . . . etc . . .!

The boss would draw heavy lines across each page of the trainee's work, throw the folder at him and end the surgery by saying 'Get out and do it again and for Pete's sake *get it right* next time . . .' The terrified and utterly demoralised trainee would slink away tail between legs wondering whether he could find another job somewhere else – many did.

The boss meanwhile saw nothing wrong with his methods of 'teaching' but would complain that here he was, desperately busy, and having to waste valuable time on fools. However, despite his pathetically inadequate performance as a teacher, this boss was a very intelligent and capable man – but permanently exhausted. Like the MDs in the *Chief Executive* survey he worked too hard, too long and was endlessly taking on too much for the good of his subordinates or himself. In other words, despite his innate abilities, he was not fit for business.

It is not only leadership skills which suffer through tiredness and the anxiety which goes hand in glove with it. Errors of calculation and judgement will occur and the ability to think clearly and positively will be diminished. The thinking behind the regulations forbidding lorry drivers or airline pilots to work more than certain hours without a rest applies equally well to every other type of work. Road accidents or plane crashes are dramatic events in which lives can be lost – hence the regulations imposed by the authorities. It is no less necessary for the executive to be subject to similar regulations which, if not self-imposed, should be laid down by the company. The health of the individual and the health of the business can depend on such controls.

Of course all business executives should be prepared to work long hours, even excessively long hours, in cases of genuine emergency. The problem is that many of the workaholics convince themselves that there is a permanent state of emergency *and* that only they can save the business. The result is often a lot of human misery, bad management, reduced profits and chaos when the workaholic retires, goes (reluctantly) on holiday or drops dead.

The solution to workaholism does not lie in exhortations

to slow down and take it easy. Most workaholics are incapable of slowing down and find periods of inactivity a form of torture. The trick is to convince them that they should do something *outside* the business which, in a different way, is equally demanding. Some ideas for such activities are provided in later pages.

21

Pushed around and anxious

ALMOST EVERYONE has a boss. He or she may be a considerate, intelligent individual who makes an effort to manage effectively and to ensure the contentment and well-being of subordinates. Alternatively, we may be stuck with a bad-tempered idiot who makes our lives a misery by one or more of the following weaknesses:

- Fails to delegate and thereby frustrates and discourages the juniors.

- Never fails to dump work (as opposed to properly planned delegation) on already overburdened people with
  (a) little or no guidance as to what is wanted or how the work should be done, and
  (b) a demand for the work to be completed 'yesterday'.

- Takes all the credit for work well done.

- Passes the blame to subordinates when something goes wrong.

- Insists on the observance of petty rules and regulations.

- Gives no support when the going is tough.

- Discourages the use of initiative and the opportunity for creative activity. 'You are not paid to think' is a favourite slogan.

- Is distant, unfriendly and frequently downright rude.

- Sees good employees as a threat and will do everything possible to discredit (or get rid of) anyone with real ability.

- Undermines subordinates by taking action on matters for which they are responsible without telling them.

- Gives orders, never consults and does not want advice or suggestions.

Anyone with a boss like this can only endure each agonising and depressing day and needs a way to combat the anxiety and unhappiness which will result. Lack of defence against such misfortune can cause the anxiety to build up to proportions which may trigger off physical ailments similar to those which can occur with people who have suffered a bereavement or a divorce.

Recent research on the effects of anxiety and depression on the body's immune system strongly suggests that there is a connection. Dentists find that mouth abscesses most frequently occur when patients are under mental pressure, and studies in America have revealed that anxiety causes the body to react. Apparently a steroid called cortisol is produced by the body when mental pressures mount up and this steroid inhibits the action of cells in the bloodstream which fight viruses and bacteria. Reports from both Ohio University and Duke University support the view that the psychological state influences physical health in a real way. The evidence is that the 'Monday morning illness' can be much more real than imagined when the job imposes anxiety on the worker. British researchers are working on this problem too, and the Cancer Research Campaign, for example, is running a 5-year programme to investigate evidence that the anxieties of cancer patients can make their physical condition worse.

For business people otherwise in good health, there are ways and means to combat the problem of the anxiety-inducing job – other than shooting the boss or moving on to greener pastures. These ideas, described later when we have covered more of the negative side to work, are in addition to the physical exercise already recommended as a way to fight stress.

22

Grossly underpaid

HUMAN NATURE and the way we all think make it a near certainty that most of us believe we are underpaid. The process which leads to this conclusion is simple and works in the following way.

Let's imagine Ted, a middle manager in a large company who is earning £15,000 pa. Ted, like everyone else, would like to take more exotic holidays, buy a new car to keep up with the guy next door and satisfy a number of other pressing 'wants'. He received a rise of £1,000 last year and, at the time, was fairly happy about it. Now he has become accustomed to his £15,000 salary and has been thinking in terms of £17,000 as a reasonable amount. At this level he could afford the new car and the exotic holiday. He is beginning to feel dissatisfied, despite the fact that he is better off than he was a year ago. That phase of his life is in the past and he is, not unreasonably, thinking about the future.

What will happen if Ted gets a further rise to bring his salary up to the £17,000 he thinks he should have? At first he will be delighted and to some extent motivated. But, after only a few weeks, he will start thinking about his next rise and may have visions of £19,000. As soon as he starts thinking about this level of income, the recently awarded £17,000 seems positively niggardly! Ted will now, gradually, convince himself that he is underpaid and will support this view by a strong suspicion that he is paid less than his colleagues. 'How is it,' he will ask himself, 'that George has been able to buy that big house on a prestige estate or Harry managed the payment on his super-charged sports car?' The answer, to Ted, will be obvious. They are paid much more than he is and, since he does the same job equally well (if not better most of the time), the whole thing is grossly unjust. Ted will now begin to feel thoroughly resentful and depressed about the whole rotten, shameful business.

In case this all sounds too over the top to be true, consider the real-life experience of Sid.

Sid, who worked as a member of a small team of computer systems analysts, went through all the feelings and suspicions ascribed to the mythical Ted. He put his case to the boss, who was not particularly sympathetic and Sid came away from the interview quite certain that he was the lowest paid member of the team – although one of the most experienced. Sid became so upset by his convictions that he waited behind after closing time one night, sneaked into the computer room and, entirely against the rules, ran the payroll through the machine. (This was in the days of punched cards when such things were easier to do.)

The computer did its stuff and Sid studied the print-out with care only to find that his salary *was* exceptional. He was the *highest* paid member of the team! After the initial shock wore off, Sid became more happy with his lot – until it occurred to him that the whole team might be underpaid. Sid began to study the job ads to see what level of salaries systems analysts were paid by other companies. Of course, he found some higher salaries on offer and the whole process of self-induced misery started all over again. Eventually Sid left to take up one of the advertised jobs, no doubt with some very temporary satisfaction with his new salary.

The point about all this is that once employees become convinced that they are being shabbily treated, they become fed up at best and 'sick with anger' at worst. In neither case are such people as effective as they would be if they were content with their salary. The problem, except in cases where salary really is at a grossly unjust level, is self-induced. The solution therefore must come from the individual with or without help from the company.

23

Left behind in the rat-race

A PROBLEM which can hit people in their forties and fifties in particular is the gradual realisation that they are not likely to go any further. A few years without promotion and seeing younger people overtaking in the hierarchal ladder can be a demoralising and depressing experience.

The overlooked executive, especially one carrying a chip on his or her shoulder, is a sad sight to behold. Such people hang around, looking more and more sad-sack as the months go by and becoming more and more grumpy. Their work suffers and, most marked of all, they are less willing to co-operate with colleagues – especially the younger ones on the way up. Since there is rarely enough room at the top for everyone who wants to get there, we are all potential casualties. The problem is a serious one, which can make the victims ill and, in one case in my experience, lead to suicide. Once again we have a situation causing mental pressure and anxiety which can manifest itself not only in poor quality work but in physical ailments as well.

These are some of the more common causes of anxiety, depression and illness which the executives face. We have already considered exercise and diet as a means to ward off a range of physical and mental ailments, but there is a third option open to us – attitude and life-style.

24

The attitude defence

As REGARDS the problems described in this part of the book, the most universally helpful attitude is:

'I will not just sit here and take it.'

Hamlet asked himself 'Whether 'tis nobler in the mind to suffer the slings and arrows of outrageous fortune, or to take arms against a sea of troubles, and by opposing end them?' Not only is it 'nobler in the mind' to fight our problems, it is also a way to get rid of them or neutralise them. What, for example, should we do about the awful boss?

The answer is certainly not to just go on passively accepting the situation. A passive attitude will change nothing. The victim can make a start by firmly pointing out to the boss how unsatisfactory everything is and how his or her way of doing things is not only making his or her life a misery but is bad for the boss too. A demoralised, demotivated department will not enhance the boss's reputation.

Such approaches to a stupid boss are not easy to make and do not always result in anything useful. If so, don't give up, but go over his head. No one should have any qualms about this, because a bad boss who knows of your unhappiness and does nothing about it deserves the trouble he is asking for. There is quite a lot of technique to be applied in fighting bad bosses, and a very useful book on the subject is *How to Fight Your Boss and Win* by Jonathan Kramer (published by Arbor House). Kramer is a clinical psychologist who describes different kinds of boss and strategies that will work with the bad ones.

If you are worried and depressed about your salary, think about it objectively. Are you merely stuck in the mental process which Ted suffered from or are you really hard done by? If the latter, do something. Prepare a sensible, balanced case and present it to the boss. Once again Kramer has some helpful advice on this topic. At all events you will no longer be suffering sleepless nights brooding over the slings and arrows of this type of misfortune.

The important thing, whatever your problem, is to take a positive attitude to it. In other words, firmly decide to do something, decide what to do and get going. Deciding *what* to do can be difficult but don't be discouraged. One helpful technique is to take a sheet of paper and write down, on one side, the factors which make up your problem. On the other side write down all the possible things you could do about these factors and, perhaps with the help of friends or colleagues, use them to work out a strategy. Merely doing this will make you feel better – simply because an aggressive approach raises hopes and provides a sense of self-respect.

The mention of self-respect brings us to another range of measures which the individual can take. These measures provide an *alternative* way to be creative; they are helpful for those who are stuck in a rut or have a restrictive boss and, in various ways, will also help the workaholic.

25

Creative alternatives

THE SLOGAN to be adopted is 'If you can't be creative at work, be creative elsewhere'. In other words, if you can't do anything to improve the work environment and it is damaging your mental and physical health, gird up your loins and find your own solution. This does not mean chucking up your job and becoming a beach bum in Florida. There are many responsible and useful things people can do to prove (at least to themselves) that they can be useful in life and achieve something to be proud of. Here are some ideas.

Working from home

In addition to the hours that must be spent at work, everyone has some spare time (all except the workaholic who must *make* spare time). There are dozens of ways in which this time can be spent running your own small business from home. Real-life cases of people who have proved their worth and made some money include the following:

- Picture framing – the man who did this as a relief from the horrors of his job now has a full-time business employing six people.

- Computer programming – a divorced woman regained her confidence by taking on private work from local firms.

- Printing – a nice little earner for a man in his fifties who realised he would get no further in his job.

- Writing – articles for business magazines which led to a contract to do book reviews.

- Catering for parties – a husband and wife enterprise which gave them both a sense of pride their dreary jobs did not provide.

All these people achieved a sense of self-fulfilment – the ultimate motivation according to Abraham Maslow, who developed the famous 'hierarchy of human needs' theory (see Appendix 1). The man who built up the picture-framing business started it purely as a hobby:

> I was not happy at work and did not get on with my boss. The general worry was making me ill and I found that I needed something to take my mind off my problems at weekends. My wife suggested a hobby and, reluctantly at first (I was not convinced a hobby would work), I started picture framing. Things went so well that after about a year I told my boss to keep the job and I have never looked back. I am happier than I have ever been and as fit as the proverbial fiddle.

Support for the idea that running your own business can be good for the health was provided, in early 1987, by a survey produced by the Small Business Research Trust. The results indicated that although the entrepreneurs often earned less than when they were employed by someone else, they were likely to be more healthy – and more healthy than their own employees. The survey also showed that the self-employed entrepreneur works long hours and yet his or her health does not necessarily suffer as a result.

This image of the self-employed (hard work and less

money) is not unfamiliar to those of us who have tried self-employment or who have friends or relatives who have done so. Why then should such people tend to be more healthy?

The strong implication is that the mental stimulation and satisfaction of being in charge and the opportunity for creativity and self-fulfilment make all the difference. The fact that the employees of people running their own businesses were found by the Trust's survey to be less healthy also supports this view!

Clearly small entrepreneurs must also learn to delegate and to give employees a 'piece of the action' if they want satisfied and healthy staff.

The pure hobby

Whether or not there is an intention to make money or develop a business, a demanding hobby can be a great way to relieve pressure. Winston Churchill took up painting, which he did badly, and bricklaying, which he did worse, but both of which no doubt gave him relief from weighty affairs of state.

Charity work can also be fulfilling and it is an ideal cure for self-pity. The solace to one's own distress can readily be found in providing help to people in greater need. The boss may do nothing but scowl when you appear but the welcoming smile from, say, an elderly housebound person receiving your help is good compensation.

There are hobbies such as rambling, bird-watching and orienteering which have an in-built degree of exercise for those who wish to combine mental relaxation with physical effort. There are others such as music which can be therapeutic without providing physical exercise. Music in particular, both to play and to listen to, 'has charms to soothe a savage breast', and is also, for those with the inclination, reputed to be 'the food of love'.

One senior and overworked executive took up choral singing as a hobby and found that he benefited mentally and physically from this activity and also found the social side a pleasant relaxation. His colleagues in the choir came from many walks of life so very few ever wanted to talk business.

These are all ways to 'get away from it all' and, by concentrating the mind on other things, help to recharge the batteries. There is one hobby, however, which in my opinion beats the lot – gardening. You may have a large enough garden to keep you busy, but for those who have only a small patch (or none at all) an allotment has a lot to offer.

The benefits of an allotment

Allotments are hard work, a fact which puts many people off the idea. There are also people who have the strange notion that gardening is somehow socially unacceptable for a business executive and only suitable for horny-handed sons (or daughters) of toil. How wrong these people are! The profit, pleasure and health-giving results of working an allotment are many and varied. Consider the following:

- Exercise. A half-hour digging session will work off some adrenaline, burn up some calories and strengthen the muscles. Even an hour's relatively gentle hoeing or sowing will provide useful exercise and get some underused muscles working.

- Profit. A standard sized allotment (about 50ft × 100ft) will produce all the vegetables the average family of mother, father and 1.8 children can eat. The cost, excluding a charge for your labour, will work out around £3–£5 a year for seeds plus a rent of about the same amount. There is no need to buy fertilizer, chemicals or anything else. The value of the produce should well exceed £200 – free of tax.

For those who consider £200 to be small beer and not worth bothering about there are other advantages to consider.

- Flavour. The taste of, say, runner beans, cooked about 30 minutes after harvesting, is out of this world and far superior to that of the frozen or tinned variety. They are also normally better than the fresh vegetables provided by the greengrocer. His vegetables are probably harvested days, even weeks, before you buy them.

- Chemical-free. If you grow your own food, you can ensure that it is 100 per cent 'natural'. If additives, pesticides, fungicides, herbicides and other chemicals matter to you, working your own allotment is a sure way to avoid them.

- Peace and quiet. No one will bother you on your allotment. No telephones will ring, no heart-stopping urgent messages will arrive from the boss – it will be just you and the vegetables. There is nothing to beat the tranquillity of an allotment on a Sunday afternoon in the spring and, with a little steady exercise, all the world's problems can seem a long way away.

- Social life. Although no one will bother you on your allotment, there are always other gardeners around if you want some company. There will always be someone to give advice and all gardeners enjoy a chat about the weather conditions (always unfavourable), germination rates (always worse than in living memory), the quality of the seed in the shops (still going down) and all the other obstacles to raising a few crops.

- Achievement. Watching your plants grow is second only in giving a sense of achievement (and sometimes astonishment) to carrying home a basket of freshly dug carrots, parsnips or whatever. Winning the battle with the elements or the greenfly can be at least as satisfying as negotiating a good business deal or achieving a new production record – often more so, because it is all yours and very real. Let's face it, quite a lot of what we struggle to achieve in our working lives is of dubious value and somehow artificial, but there is nothing artificial about a compliment from 'old Fred' (every allotment has an old Fred who has been gardening for at least 100 years) on the quality of your onions.

Further achievement and satisfaction can be gained by trying out your own ways of sowing, planting, crop rotation and preparing the ground. Growing vegetables is not difficult and there are ample opportunities for experimentation and trying your own ideas.

Satisfaction can also be gained from planning your work (using business planning techniques) and from recycling. For example if all the weeds, household refuse, leaves and other organic junk are composted, it should not be necessary to buy fertilizer. Even old newspapers can contribute to next year's lunches if these are torn up and added to the compost.

All these benefits can come from an allotment, and in summary amount to:

Exercise
Good food
Relaxation
Achievement

Perhaps it is no accident that professional gardeners seem to live to a ripe old age more often than people in other professions.

A touch of class

For those seeking psychological fitness, in particular by developing a sense of fulfilment which may be lacking in the job, setting out on a 'learning process' can be beneficial. There is a wide variety of opportunities (and challenges) open to those seeking mental stimulation and/or a means to achieve something. These opportunities include the following.

Evening classes

Courses are available in everything from archeology to Zen Buddhism and the choice can be made to meet such needs as:

- Pure relaxation.

- Learning in order to practise a hobby.

- Acquiring a social skill, e.g. bridge-playing.

- Acquiring a money-making skill, e.g. antiques restoration.

- Improving job skills, e.g. computing.

- Preparing for a retirement job.

or an evening class may simply provide a change of scene and an opportunity to meet new people.

Anyone feeling 'stale' at work (including the workaholic) can be stimulated by one or two evenings each week tackling something entirely new. A course in archaeology, music appreciation, psychology, furniture design or anything else far removed from the business scene can provide a way out of the rut and get the brain working. The mental stimulation gained is likely to show itself at work in the form of improved alertness and general enthusiasm.

For those people seeking a greater sense of fulfilment,

classes which lead to examinations can provide this. Such was the case with Terence who, at the age of about 30, found himself slipping behind his colleagues and realised that he was suffering from the disadvantage of having no formal qualifications. Although good at his job, he was not 'taken seriously' by his boss, who was obsessed with the idea that only qualified accountants were capable of handling the management consultancy work of the department. Terence became fed up and bored with the trivial projects given to him and signed up at a polytechnic for evening classes leading to a Diploma in Management Studies. After much hard work (which he enjoyed) Terence obtained his diploma and, a year later, changed jobs. He is now personnel director of a major company and gets all the fulfilment he needs.

Another possibility for suitably qualified people is to look for a job as a teacher at an evening institute. For those with the aptitude for it, teaching can be a rewarding and satisfying activity. John, an underwriter with a large insurance company, found teaching the answer to his particular problems. Although well qualified in insurance, he was not regarded by his employers as management material and was never given responsibility for other people. As the years went by John became depressed by this and, as he said:

I was becoming the oldest insurance technician in the business. I should have taken on responsibility for a department as my contemporaries had done and spent my time leading and controlling the juniors. Instead I was doing routine work and becoming more and more unhappy as the years went by. My heart was not in the job and when I began to find myself in trouble for making silly mistakes I knew that things had gone too far. My wife, who could see how low I had become, suggested I should teach classes for the institute examinations which I had passed myself many years before. I approached a college and somewhat to my surprise was promptly given a job teaching two evenings a week. This has changed my life out of all recognition and when my students pass their exams I feel on top of the world. I also enjoy my two evenings out each week – the students are young and make me feel young too.

Open University

Another real-life story comes from Bob, who reached a middle management level at the age of 45 but realised by the time he was 50 that any further promotion was most unlikely.

I was head of the design department but just knowing that I would be stuck there for the next 15 years made me look on it more as a prison sentence than a career. I did not want to deteriorate into an embittered has-been and I was still ambitious. I started an Open University course and never looked back.

Bob obtained a degree from the OU, and at 55 took an opportunity to retire early. He knew from his performance on the OU course that he could do something more challenging. Early retirement gave him the opportunity. He sold his house in the Home Counties and bought a former rectory in Somerset. Bob then spent a year converting this large old building into holiday flats and now runs a flourishing business of his own. 'It's not just a case of marching them in and taking the money', he says. 'I grow vegetables in the garden which they buy, I organise riding and other holiday activities and there is quite a lot of forward planning to be done. It's much more fun than going on being chief designer for years and years.'

Alternative possibilities which an OU course might bring are:

● Improved 'market value' and a new job.

- Better performance in the present job.

- Promotion on the strength of having new knowledge and skills.

- More interest in life all round.

Short full-time courses

There are a number of organisations providing short courses (weekends or a full week), which, if holiday time can be spared, can be both refreshing and helpful. Of course if your company is enlightened enough to give time off for a course, so much the better. However, I am not referring here to business subject courses (valuable though they can be) but to a non-vocational course chosen for its therapeutic effect.

Managements might well consider a short sabbatical for employees who are showing signs of stress and give them the time off and pay their expenses. Even a few days in new surroundings, applying the mind, body or both to a totally new subject, can be an excellent way to reduce stress and anxiety. A normal holiday is not the same, since the stressed employee has ample time to exercise his or her mind thinking about work problems; and lying on a sunny beach worried sick about work problems is not much different from worrying about them in the office or factory – except that on holiday there is more time to do it.

One organisation which provides a good range of short courses is The Earnley Concourse, Chichester, Sussex. Over periods ranging from 2 to 5 days students can immerse themselves in subjects such as languages, various arts and crafts, writing (e.g. short stories), calligraphy, computer programming, physical fitness, swimming and listening techniques. Some of the skills taught may have an application in the workplace, but the primary purpose for someone needing to be fit for business is therapeutic.

Another organisation which offers some helpful courses

is the School of Continuing Education at The University of Kent, Canterbury. The school runs a 'Summer Academy' programme comprising week-long study holidays at a number of universities throughout the country. Experienced university tutors will introduce students to archaeology (including an examination of Hadrian's wall), architecture and many aspects of the arts and literature.

These then are some of the ways to improve mental fitness, and they could perhaps form part of the programme of someone who wishes to obtain all-round improvement. A weekly evening class in, say, art appreciation could be complementary to a regular Saturday morning swimming session.

Self-induced stress

There is always the possibility that any stress you may suffer from does not result from a bad boss but from your own way of working. John, a conscientious executive, had a supportive and intelligent boss but despite this became ill with stress symptoms. He had two weeks away from work to rest but only a few weeks later he went sick again. A careful examination of the circumstances surrounding John's problem revealed that he was continually struggling to meet deadlines and never seemed to be able to control his work – it was controlling him. It was clear that John was permanently in a muddle with one priority being piled on another, resulting in considerable worry and fear of failure. The whole situation was made worse by his conscientiousness which, at least in his own mind, exaggerated the seriousness of every crisis.

The solution was to send John on a time management course during which he was taught how to organise himself and establish priorities. Such courses can show people how to work more effectively and thus avoid creating their own stress.

The subjects which can be usefully learned include:

- Identifying the important as opposed to the urgent work and establishing a work list for each day with priorities placed in order.

- Delegation methods, e.g. how to make better use of your secretary.

- Eliminating unnecessary tasks or time-wasting activities.

Learning these techniques and following them up with *disciplined* practice – it is only too easy to slip back into bad old habits – can be the answer to anxiety and the ill health which can result.

26

Pampering yourself

A NUMBER of 'treatments' that can be taken are claimed by some people to be positively curative. Sauna baths, for instance, are said by some to cure rheumatism. Others will say that a sauna bath will 'tone up the muscles' or 'drive toxins from the body'. Few people who have tried it will disagree with the view that a sauna session can make one feel relaxed – even if it cures nothing and if all the sweating does nothing for the 'toxins in the body'.

There is also the argument that anything you do which makes you feel good will do you good even if the effect is purely psychological. If the problem is psychological and relief is achieved by enjoying some form of treatment, which at best can be regarded as pampering, then it is worth serious consideration. Let's take a look at some of these slightly hedonistic possibilities.

Sauna baths

The Scandinavians have been using sauna baths for the best part of 2,000 years and show no sign of losing their enthusiasm. Since the Scandinavians are down-to-earth people not given to wasting time and money on 'nonsense', there must be something to be gained from the sauna other than just becoming cleaner.

Some physical effects of a sauna are clear:

- The steam and high temperature open the pores and promote sweating.

- The muscles are relaxed by the heat.

The claims made for these demonstrable physical effects are that:

- Blood pressure is reduced.

- The mind is relaxed.

Whether or not these claims are correct, many people take saunas because they *feel* better afterwards. Some claim to feel invigorated by the sauna and some use it as a means to refresh themselves before a difficult meeting or after a long day – perhaps with more problems to face.

A sauna then is worth trying but a few simple rules should be observed:

- If you are not accustomed to saunas, don't stay too long. The heat can be quite fierce (50+ degrees Celsius) and, at first, just a few minutes are advisable. When more accustomed to the heat after a number of sessions, the time spent can be increased to about 15 minutes. At all events leave the sauna cabin if you feel uncomfortable.

- Cool off cautiously. Very fit people may take a cold plunge after leaving the sauna but this can be quite a shock to the body. A mildly warm shower is probably better.

  One victim of the after-sauna shock was a British holidaymaker in Finland who died after leaping into an icy lake immediately after leaving the sauna. However, the unfortunate victim was a young man who shared the sauna with three Finnish girls, a fact which may have added some strain to his system.

- Don't use the sauna if you are feeling unwell, have a history of heart problems, are pregnant or after drinking alcohol.

- Don't use the sauna after a heavy meal.

Some people use saunas as part of a slimming campaign but this is not a way to lose weight permanently. There will be some weight loss due to perspiration but this goes straight back on with the next drink.

Steam baths

The steam bath differs from the sauna in that temperatures are lower and the humidity higher. The high humidity promotes sweating and deep cleaning effects. Some people find the lower temperature of the steam bath preferable to the relatively fierce heat of the sauna and find that they gain the same therapeutic effects.

Whirlpool baths

The whirlpool bath massages the body with jets of water. This, it is said, relaxes the body and eases tension in tired muscles.

Similar claims are made (mostly by the manufacturers) for whirlpools as for saunas, plus the claim that the high water temperature speeds up the metabolism. Whether or not these alleged benefits can be substantiated, the whirlpool bath does provide a relaxed, comfortable feeling, and if it is refreshing, either mentally or physically, the effect must be good. People with backache or strained muscles may find the whirlpool helpful, particularly if the jets can be adjusted to play on the affected part of the body.

Although a whirlpool will never be as hot as a sauna, it can still take some getting used to. It is wise therefore not to take too long a session – and none at all after alcohol, a heavy meal or if unwell. Anyone with urinary incontinence problems or thrush should not use whirlpools at all, as not only will other users be placed at risk but these conditions can be worsened by the chemicals added to the water.

Aromatherapy

The ancient Egyptians rubbed themselves with oil in which various plants had been soaked as a treatment for physical and psychological problems. This ancient treatment, which is alive and well under the name of aromatherapy, uses distilled oils obtained from various plants.

The Greeks, Romans and Persians also practised aromatherapy, using it as a cure for a variety of ailments. During the eighteenth and nineteenth centuries such treatments went out of fashion as medical practitioners began to use the man-made drugs which were becoming available to them. In recent years aromatherapy has reappeared as a form of alternative medicine, partly as a result of an accidental discovery made in France in the 1920s. A French chemist named Gattefosse burned his hand and, to obtain relief from the pain, plunged it into some lavender oil. To his surprise the burn healed much more quickly than he expected and no scar was formed. This may have been due simply to the cooling effect of the oil and have had nothing whatever to do with any healing properties of lavender. However, the incident stimulated interest in the use of various oils derived from plants and aromatherapy is now a thriving industry.

Aromatherapists claim that the plant oils can be beneficial in treating psychological as well as physical conditions, including stress and depression. Rosemary and camomile are said to relieve tiredness and irritability, lavender to have sedative properties and rosewood to be stimulating. Sandalwood, it is claimed, will cheer you up in times of sadness.

By no means everyone believes these claims and some medical experts refute them. However, a session at an aromatherapy clinic can at least promote a sense of relaxation and well-being, and this alone may be enough to raise the spirits to an acceptable level for business efficiency. More information on Aromatherapy is provided in Appendix 2.

Massage

There are various types of massage, the most common being the so-called 'Swedish massage', which applies fairly firm but steady pressure on the whole body, including the feet. Other forms of massage include pummelling of the muscles, and in the Japanese version considerable pressure can be applied to various parts of the body. In a genuine Japanese bath house, the masseuse (never a masseur) will apply pressure with the fingertips which can be quite painful – and by kneeling on the patient's back apply pressure which can be very painful! However, the Japanese masseuses receive a long training, and this acute form of pressure is skilfully applied to carefully selected areas, with the effect of loosening tense tissue.

All forms of massage, given by a trained practitioner, will result in a relaxed feeling and can ease stiffness, aches and pains. Claims are made that massage 'eases muscular tension', reduces blood pressure and 'tones up the muscles'. Quite what the latter statement means is open for debate but, like aromatherapy, if massage makes someone feel good, then the effect is good. Many people do find massage a way to relieve anxiety and stress.

Perhaps the best of all possible worlds can be obtained by a combination of treatments. The tense, anxious executive could start with a sauna bath, followed with a shower and go on to a session of aromatherapy. Since the aromatherapy will include massage, the combined effect of this sequence must surely be relaxing. The really hedonistic could add a whirlpool bath for good measure.

Acupressure

Not quite in the realms of 'pampering yourself', this treatment is somewhat similar to acupuncture but without the puncture. No needles are used and, instead, pressure is applied to various part of the body with the fingertips. Acupressure is said to relieve pain, tension and stress and to 'invigorate the system'.

Ionithermie

Normally promoted as a beauty treatment, ionithermie is also said to improve circulation and promote muscle firmness. This treatment is popular as a means to remove facial wrinkles and is believed by some to be a slimming treatment.

Sleep and lack of it

The amount of sleep needed to work effectively varies greatly from one person to another. However, lack of the amount you need will have a deleterious effect on your work and, if prolonged, on your health.

Problems loom larger when we are tired and work which may, after a good night's sleep, be bearable or even enjoyable can become a dreary grind. The fit executive will avoid, as far as possible, the mid-week party and sacrifice the late night TV movie if either of these will result in obtaining less sleep than is needed. It is not uncommon to find that the 'fed-up with everything' executive is actually burning the candle at both ends either by overworking or over-playing or both.

Summary

1. Anyone can become fed up with his/her job and many will suffer anxiety and stress for one reason or another. These results of dissatisfaction can result in poor health.

2. Poor management of the individual by low quality bosses can be a significant problem.

3. Real or imagined unfairness in pay and lack of promotion can also lead to ill health.

4. There are several defences, including:

   - Developing a non-passive attitude and learning to attack the problem.

   - Finding creative opportunities outside the work environment.

   - Learning new skills either for pure relaxation or to improve 'market value'.

   - Planning your work to avoid self-induced stress.

   - 'Pampering yourself' with the use of treatments which may be physically therapeutic but which are almost certainly mentally therapeutic.

5. Lack of sleep does nothing for your health and can contribute to feeling fed-up. A good night's sleep makes our problems seem less intractable.

PART 5

Fit for Travel

27

Is travel fun?

IF THERE is one aspect of business life which requires a fair degree of fitness, travel is it. The combined effects of hanging around at airports, jet-lag, unfamiliar (or inedible) food and the sheer exhaustion of repeated business meetings can be very demanding. The 1-day train trip is bearable, if frustrating at times, and although the traveller can arrive home feeling thoroughly drained after a day trip, it is the foreign trip lasting, say, 2 or more weeks, which can be a real challenge.

People who never travel overseas on business often seem to imagine that the business trip is no more than a free holiday. 'How lucky you are to go to all those exciting places,' one non-traveller remarked to me just before I set off on a 3½ week trip to the USA and the Caribbean. My own reaction at the end of it all was how nice it was to get home from a trip in which, for unavoidable reasons, I had changed time zone six times – and felt it.

The trip had made quite a number of other demands on my mental and physical ability which regular travellers will be only too familiar with:

- Lugging a heavy suitcase and a mountain of files in and out of hotels, taxis and airports.

- A boring 12 hours in a plane from Heathrow to San Francisco, as a start to the trip.

- Breakfast meetings (ugh!) with workaholic clients who want to demonstrate how busy they are and how fast they can think just after dawn has broken.

- Lunch and dinner meetings with yet more clients.

- Hotel menu fatigue.

- Sudden and frustrating changes of schedule – 'Sorry, can't manage Tuesday morning after all. Can we make it Wednesday morning instead?' Wednesday is of course the only day convenient to at least four other people and it will now be necessary to book a late-night flight to the next city on the list.

- White-knuckle landings and takeoffs and periods of sheer terror as homicidal taxi drivers weave through the motorway traffic (steering one-handed of course).

Add to these items the extra-busy days of negotiation, presentations and dealing with problems, and the whole thing is rather less than a holiday, free or otherwise.

Some travellers find an additional strain in being alone on a trip, not just because periods of feeling lonely can occur but also because there is no friendly colleague to discuss problems with. Keeping problems in perspective when over-tired, over-fed and sitting alone in yet another dreary hotel room can be difficult, to say the least. If, on top of all this, the traveller goes down with a dose of Montezuma's revenge (otherwise known as traveller's tummy, Bombay belly and squitters), then life can be pretty awful.

Despite all these horrors which can face the business traveller, there are many ways to make the trip more bearable and even a pleasure. A successful trip begins with the preparations for it.

28

Preparation and prevention

The schedule

EVERYONE HAS a mental and physical limit, which, once reached, is the beginning of a rapid fall-off in performance. Some people can keep going, producing good results, for several weeks. Others begin to cave in after a few days. The first requirement is to recognise one's limitations and, as far as possible, plan the trip accordingly.

There is a temptation to, say, cross the Atlantic and, having paid the fare, to cram in every possible visit from Montreal to Mexico City. This can be a serious mistake, since on a long trip, perhaps with valuable business at stake, the cost of the trans-Atlantic flight can be insignificant. In many cases it makes more sense to do some good work, fly home for a rest and have another go later. Extending a trip too long can result in poor work and lost sales.

It is also important to choose the start day carefully and to plan ahead for weekends. Many business travellers leave home on a Sunday in order to 'save time' and be ready to start work on Monday. Many people also try to use weekend time for moving from city to city, again to save working time. The result of this is to allow the combined effect of jet-lag and general fatigue to have a maximum adverse effect on efficiency.

If business is to start on a Monday, it is better to leave home on the previous Friday in order to have time to get over the jet-lag and, in appropriate cases, to become accustomed to sudden changes in climate or altitude. By doing so, there is a better prospect of being fit for business on the Monday morning.

A further advantage of spending the weekend at one's destination is that it allows you time to 'scout around', find out where the places to be visited are located and pick up useful local knowledge. For example, it is worth finding out that it is impossible to hail a taxi in the street in Vancouver. This can be a problem if discovered too late when rushing from one appointment to another.

Even if the flight is within much the same time zone (e.g. London to Johannesburg), the body will have been cramped into an aircraft seat for a number of hours. The opportunity to take some brisk walks over the weekend will be valuable in restoring the body and spirits.

Using the weekends for rest and relaxation during a trip is also important. If weekends are needed at home to restore efficiency, they are even more necessary during a demanding trip. Ideally any change of city will be completed on the Friday afternoon so that the Saturday and Sunday are free. In countries where either Saturday or Sunday are working days the normal local rest days should be allowed for instead. These rest days can be used in any way preferred but if possible something with a purpose should be chosen. One non-demanding and usually interesting activity is to take a conducted coach trip to see the local sights. In most places tours lasting from 2 hours to whole weekends are available, and they are normally designed to include the maximum of interest with the minimum of mileage. A useful mixture is, say, a half-day tour, some walking round the shops, a session in the hotel swimming pool or multi-gym and some quiet reading or review of the files required for the days ahead.

Other aspects of planning the schedule to avoid the problems of overdoing it are:

- Limiting appointments to three or four a day. If making any kind of 'in depth' presentation, adequate time must be allowed. Dashing breathless from one meeting to another is neither efficient or likely to keep the traveller in good condition.

- Allowing contingency time. Things will go wrong and sometimes additional meetings will crop up, however carefully the planning has been done. Allowing a 'free hour' by scheduling the last appointment for 4.00 in Western countries and 2.30 in tropical countries can provide time to deal with the unexpected – or provide a welcome break.

- Allowing ample time to get to the airports. A last-minute mad rush adds to the stress, and if the plane is missed, a lot of stress can be caused.

- Avoiding 'collecting countries'. There are individuals whose main purpose when travelling on business seems to be to add stamps to their passports. One exponent of this form of ego trip travelled from Geneva to Nairobi via Ethiopia. Since there was no business to be done in Ethiopia and it is hardly a desirable holiday spot, it can only be assumed that his 2 day stop-over was to give him something to boast about.

   Such people, and those who brag about having circumnavigated the globe three times in 2½ days ('only had 2 hours in Karachi before I had to dash on to Bombay') are a menace to themselves and the business they work for. No one can be effective when exhausted by such crazy schedules.

Survival kit

Obviously the traveller must carry an adequate supply of any prescribed medicines. In addition, a small supply of other medicinal items can make all the difference between a sucessful trip and one ruined by illness. In some countries medicines for minor ailments are not always readily available, and even in countries where they are available, the chances are that they will be urgently needed when all the shops are shut. The following is a list of recommended items to take with you:

- *Pain killers*. Your preferred tablets for headache and toothache may well be needed. From time to time every traveller wakes up with a headache or, worse, toothache. This will occur on the morning when a crucial early meeting has been arranged and the hotel shop does not open in time to sell you the remedy.

- *Alka-Seltzer*. Quite as debilitating as headache or toothache, an upset stomach will occur from time to time. Alka-Seltzer (or a similar product) is a good neutraliser and will often deal with the nausea caused by an unaccustomed diet or whatever.

- *Imodium*. This product, available without prescription, is an effective remedy for diarrhoea. The onset of this complaint can be sudden and embarrassing and can spell disaster on a day of important meetings. It is also a thoroughly nasty problem to deal with when on a long flight. Aircraft toilet facilities are not the best available for the diarrhoea sufferer and you can bet your boots that the worst attacks will occur during times of air turbulence when the traveller must remain strapped to his or her seat.

- *Band-aid*. Some form of sticking plaster plus a small tube of antiseptic cream can be a life-saver. Small cuts and grazes are at best a nuisance and in tropical countries can turn septic in a matter of hours. Quick, self-administered treatment can prevent a lot of trouble and discomfort.

- *Anti-malaria tablets*. Malaria can kill and should be treated with the utmost respect. Anyone travelling to, *or through*, an area where malaria is endemic should take the appropriate precautions. Some form of prophylaxis in the shape of tablets should be taken at the specified intervals, starting *before* leaving the home base. The tablets should be continued after arriving home again, as the malaria parasite stays in the blood stream for some time. Professional medical advice should be sought on the tablets to be used, how frequently to take them and when to start and stop.

- *Vaccination and inoculation.* The old bogey, smallpox, has been eliminated and we no longer need to be vaccinated and carry the old yellow vaccination record card. However, there are other nasty diseases against which precautions must be taken, including yellow fever and typhoid. Once again medical advice should be sought.

  Examples of the requirements for various countries are provided in Appendix 11.

A tussle with the dentist

Toothache has already been mentioned as a debilitating disaster when far from home and one's dentist. It may of course be possible to obtain quick and skilled treatment from a local dentist but, on the other hand, it may not. In some places dental treatment is primitive or non-existent, whilst in others it is available but absurdly expensive.

At best the onset of toothache can result in distracting pain or discomfort and time lost obtaining treatment. Prevention is clearly the best approach and, even if the dentist is regularly seen for routine check-ups, it can be worth a special session before a long trip. It should not be forgotten that only slight difficulties can be magnified by local conditions in some exotic places. Although minor gum recession, for instance, may not be a serious problem in a temperate climate, it can be extremely painful elsewhere. The cold air in Scandinavia or Canada during the winter months can turn a sensitive tooth into a source of severe pain, which some simple treatment before leaving home can prevent.

29

Coping with air travel

FLIGHTS OF only 1 or 2 hours' duration are not particularly exhausting, although any apprehension over take-offs and landings can take some of the stuffing out of the traveller. The big problem is the long flight (6 hours or more), especially if made across the lines of longitude. This lengthy, east–west or west–east travel is the real bugbear of the business traveller, because the combination of time change and sheer tedium can be seriously debilitating. Not only is the body's 'biological clock' thrown into confusion but the traveller can also suffer from dehydration, lost sleep and the cramping effect of sitting still for hours on end.

Most flights from the USA to London, for instance, leave at around 8.00 pm, US time, and arrive in the early morning, London time. The passenger will at best manage about 4 hours' sleep and will arrive in London at the start of the business day by no means in a fit state to handle it.

Some people find it virtually impossible to sleep on planes. Others who can sleep are likely to be woken up for dinner, breakfast, sundry announcements and even to be offered a blanket! There is no certain solution to these problems, and since different people react in different ways each individual must find his or her own remedies.

The following ideas have been gleaned from the experience of regular travellers and one or more of them may be helpful to others:

Class of travel

The company budget may determine whether someone can travel first class, club class or tourist. Within such constraints it is wise to travel in the highest class possible. The extra space provided in first and club class does allow the passenger room to stretch the legs and to avoid the uncomfortable 'elbows in' posture required in tourist seats. The company which saves money by insisting on employees enduring the more Spartan travelling conditions is likely to be making a mistake. A number of hours hunched up with elbows tucked into the sides, enduring the din of screaming children and noisy back-packers, is not a good preliminary to doing business.

Keep eating to a minimum

If your body thinks it is 3.00 am and you consume a heavy four-course meal loaded with calories, something has to give.

Avoid alcohol and smoking

The atmosphere on modern jets is a dry one and encourages dehydration. Alcohol also promotes dehydration, making the problem worse as more alcohol is consumed. In addition, the ability of the liver to process alcohol is reduced by the effect of cabin pressure and the chance of a hangover is several times higher than it is on the ground. Mineral water is the best choice when thirsty.

Cabin pressure increases the absorption of carbon dioxide in cigarette smoke and this can lead to headaches and a sense of lethargy. If you must smoke, at least cut it down.

Move about as much as possible

This will help to maintain the circulation in the body and prevent swollen feet and ankles.

Take vitamin C tablets before take off

Some people find this helpful and it has been claimed that additional vitamin C increases the oxygen level in the body tissue.

Wear loose, comfortable clothing

A thin polo neck sweater or loose shirt is preferable to the more constricting business suit. Some people recommend a ski-suit or jogging suit for air travel and some take along a pair of slippers. If the airline provides slippers, they are worth using. Synthetic materials should be avoided, as they can become too hot and rapidly become rather smelly.

Take a shower before leaving for the airport

After a few hours on a plane almost everyone begins to feel uncomfortably grubby. The chances are that the suitcase-lugging struggle to the airport and the wearisome queuing and waiting will add to the grubby feeling. Taking a last-minute shower at least starts you off feeling fresh and delays the 'grubbiness threshold'.

Sleep as much as possible

When asleep, the traveller is insulated from mental pressures, is not conscious of the tedium and is resting.

Rationalise fears

Most people, to some degree, are afraid of flying and 10 to 1 there will be a well publicised air crash just before your journey is due to start. Fear of flying ranges from mild anxiety during take-off, landing and periods of turbulence to a serious condition known as aerophobia. This condition amounts to an irrational anxiety which can develop from a sense of panic into nausea, giddiness, raised blood pressure and, at worst, heart failure.

It is generally believed that fear of flying is greater when tired or suffering from personal or business stress – which is another good reason to plan journeys to allow adequate rest periods.

Relief from aerophobia can be gained by keeping in mind the following facts:

(i)   Everyone else on board will be anxious too – some
      far more than you. The nervous passenger need
      have no sense of shame or believe that he or she is the
      only one in a cold sweat.
      I was once, for no particular reason, feeling 'nervy'
      on a long flight when I realised that the man sitting
      next to me was trembling. It was later revealed that he
      was a pilot, who told me, 'I am OK when on the flight
      deck but as a passenger I am as nervous as a kitten.' I
      felt better immediately I heard that comment and
      realised that even professional aviators can be
      nervous without any real reason.

(ii) The pilot and the crew have a vested interest in
      getting there safely too, and if, with their experience,
      they undertook the journey, the passengers need not
      be worried.

(iii) The statistics are all on your side. The fact that every
      airline accident receives massive media publicity is an
      indication of how statistically rare such events are.
      The additional fact that flight insurance for many
      thousands of pounds can be bought at airports for a
      few pounds shows how safe air travel really is.

Considering these facts and realising that flying is safer
than driving a car on a motorway can help to reduce fear
and the mental and physical exhaustion that fear can cause.
If all else fails, try a tranquilliser or a sleeping pill.

30

On the ground

Your choice of hotel

FOLLOWING YOUR arrival and the inevitable struggle through immigration and customs, you will, perhaps after a hair-raising taxi journey, arrive at your hotel. Choosing hotels is an important part of keeping yourself fit for business.

Once again company budget constraints may limit your choice of hotel but consolation can be gained from the fact that the most expensive ones are not always the best ones for the business traveller. The ideal hotel will have the following attributes:

- Location will be within walking distance of most of the places to be visited. This will not only relieve you of finding taxis and the worry that traffic jams will result in turning up late for appointments but will also provide you an opportunity for some exercise. A few minutes' walk between appointments will keep the circulation moving, provide some fresh air and give the opportunity to cogitate on the job to be done.

  Of course in some cities walking can be dangerous and in others there is the problem of being pursued by beggars, street traders and thieves and such conditions are best allowed for.

- The hotel will provide a health centre with facilities such as swimming pool, gymnasium, sauna and massage. These facilities will provide the opportunity to take some exercise and/or indulge in some 'pampering'. An early morning swim of, say, 20 minutes, will boost the metabolic rate and encourage a sense of well-being and confidence before facing the day's challenges. A sauna and massage can help with unwinding at the end of the day and encourage a good night's sleep.

- A country location for weekend accommodation. Travellers who do not mind changing hotels will find that a country location can have much to offer. Among the problems of the city centre weekend are:

  (i)   People you would prefer not to see can get at you and ruin your rest days.

  (ii) The noise and generally pressured atmosphere of the city centre are still there.

Some travellers will prefer the hustle and bustle of a city centre, but for those who welcome peace and quiet and a slower pace of life the out-of-town location could be ideal. An example would be to move out of Manhattan on Friday afternoon and stay in one of the many attractive small towns in upstate New York. Country hotels with facilities nearby for fishing, riding or simply long walks can be better places for recharging the batteries than city hotels.

Airport hotels, whilst out of town, do not normally offer these facilities, but, instead, are often characterised by noise, poor service, bad food and the smell of unburnt jet fuel.

Exercise at a pinch

Many business trips are so busy that even the best hotel exercise facilities remain unused, owing to lack of time and opportunity. If the pool is not open before 8.00 am and the first meeting starts at 8.15 am, there is no chance of a morning swim. Similarly, if the exercise facilities close down at 9.00 pm and the traveller staggers back to the hotel at midnight (having spent the evening entertaining customers), the only apparent prospect is to take a shower and fall, thankfully, into bed. In such cases the temptation to skip exercise can be hard to resist – but should be resisted. With a very full programme, exercise is even more important than ever, for as the accumulated effect of work pressure and heavy eating builds up, so efficiency declines.

The solution, apart from avoiding the heavy eating as much as possible, is to take some exercise (even a few minutes will help) each morning immediately after getting out of bed. An exercise session just before retiring can also be beneficial but it should not be strenuous on a stomach full of food and alcohol.

A good work-out can be had without equipment and the following sequence is suggested. Start gently, warming up with these stretching exercises:

- Turn the head from side to side (don't jerk) five times in each direction. Then rotate the head five times clockwise and five times anti-clockwise.

- Standing straight with arms to the side, raise and lower the shoulders ten times.

- Swing the arms together in a circular motion, brushing the ears on the upswing and the thighs on the downswing. Do ten circles forwards and ten backwards.

- Raise the arms in front of the body until parallel to the floor. Now describe small circles with each arm for 20 seconds.

- Do the same with the arms extended sideways.

- With legs apart, bend forward and try to touch the floor with the fingertips. When bent as far forward as possible and a 'pull' is felt in the legs, hold the position for a count of five and then unbend. Repeat ten times. (NB: There is no particular merit in actually managing to touch the floor. The benefit is gained by stretching until a pull is felt in the legs.)

- Repeat the previous exercise but this time reaching first for the left foot with both hands and then the right foot.

- Standing with legs apart and hands on hips, turn the trunk first to the left (as far as you can go) and then to the right. Repeat ten times.

- Raise first the left knee as high as you can, lower it and raise the right. Repeat ten times.

- Lie on your back and raise the left leg about 6 inches from the floor. Hold it for a count of 5 and lower it. Do this ten times and then repeat with the right leg.

- Stand upright and alternately rotate each foot clockwise and anticlockwise ten times in each direction.

By this stage most of the muscles will have been made to work and will be loosened. The session can now be continued with some strengthening exercises which will get the heart and lungs going as well:

- With the feet well anchored under the bed or any other convenient piece of furniture, do six sit-ups. This exercise should be done *with the legs bent*. The hands can be clasped behind the head or held forward of the body. The latter position is an easier one for those who find this exercise difficult.

- Do six press-ups, keeping the body straight and moving the arms through their full range.

- Stand upright with feet together and then slowly squat. After 2 or 3 seconds push the body upright again. Repeat six times.

This programme, *which should be adjusted according to your level of fitness*, will shake up the cobwebs and get the day off to a good start. After a refreshing shower you should be ready for action.

Eating and drinking

It is often very difficult during business travel to avoid too much food and too much booze. This is especially the case when being entertained, for refusal to try the local delicacies and specialities can cause offence. There are occasions when the traveller's host or hostess has either gone to a lot of trouble to prepare a sumptuous meal or is anxious to see the traveller enjoy the specialities of a local restaurant. The result is often a massive surplus of calories and more alcohol than can be comfortably handled. Careful selection of items from the menu (as suggested in Part 3) will not always be possible, so what other alternatives are there for keeping the situation under control? The following ideas have been found to work in practice:

(i) Make up for over-indulgence by eating very sparingly when eating alone. If, for instance, a working lunch is planned, then breakfast can be limited to, say, coffee, fruit juice and a slice of toast.

   Likewise, when free to do so, limit the evening meal to toast, soup or even cornflakes! Room service can often be persuaded to produce something very light even if the hotel restaurant is inflexible. I did, however, once persuade a waitress in a Los Angeles hotel restaurant to provide me with a dinner of porridge (or oatmeal as it is called in the USA) and much enjoyed it as a relief from the rich meals I had been consuming. The waitress derived some amusement from my choice so we were both happy.

Alternatively, if time permits, it may be possible to find a small local restaurant offering light snacks.

(ii)　At the end of a day when alcohol has been consumed, drink a glass or two of mineral water before going to bed. This will combat the alcohol-induced dehydration which contributes to hangovers and will also help your liver in its detoxification process. If, instead of working your way through the pre-dinner cocktails, wine and brandy, you can, without causing offence, stick to something innocuous like tonic water, so much the better.

The other main hazard of eating and drinking is the danger of picking up a bug which results in diarrhoea or, worse, dysentery. Dysentery can be a killer, if not treated, and even with prompt treatment can result in a lot of discomfort and lack of energy. Much of the problem comes from contaminated water and, unless the local water is known to be safe to drink, stick to bottled mineral water. This precaution should be taken in all Third World countries and no faith should be placed in hotel claims that water provided at meals or in bedrooms is boiled. The ice cubes are also suspect as the chances are that they have been made from untreated tap water. Shellfish are another likely source of trouble, and in countries where human excrement is used as fertilizer, salads are best avoided.

Other safety rules in Third World countries include:

- Choosing well cooked food.

- Choosing fruit such as bananas and oranges which you can peel yourself.

- Insisting on freshly baked bread.

Heatstroke and heat exhaustion

I once played rugby in Northern Nigeria a few days after arriving there from England. Although I was warned not to dash about as I would in England, I overdid it and spent 3 days on a bed in a darkened room recovering from heat exhaustion. This condition is normally caused by marked dehydration and salt loss as a result of copious sweating.

Vulnerability to heat exhaustion is much reduced as time goes by and acclimatisation takes place. Business trips, however, are usually too short to allow much acclimatisation and the traveller must take care not to rush about too much or for too long. It is not, by the way, necessary to play rugby to suffer heat exhaustion – a day rushing about from office to office can do it if the temperature and humidity are high.

Heatstroke, which is more serious, is caused by a sudden increase in body temperature. It can be brought about by any violent activity especially if wearing clothing which is too heavy or too constricting for the climate. Wearing appropriate clothing is therefore another precaution, and light, airy items will be safer and more comfortable. Synthetic fibres should be avoided, as they tend to be hotter, do not soak up perspiration and can encourage prickly heat. This very uncomfortable complaint (a raised skin rash which itches intolerably) is a constant hazard in humid climates. Lightweight cotton clothing combined with regular lukewarm baths or showers is the best form of prevention and also reduces the chances of heat exhaustion.

Coping with the cold

In Stockholm in winter business people can be seen wearing woolly hats and in North America ear muffs are regularly seen. In Eastern Europe thick fur hats with ear flaps are used. The English, accustomed to a temperate climate and conscious of personal appearance, arrive in very cold places wearing a winter raincoat and without a hat. It is far better to dress like a native, stay warm and avoid frost-bite in the ears.

Drugs and other temptations

Experienced business travellers are well aware that the popular image of itinerant executives spending much of their time in night clubs and brothels is grossly exaggerated. Time pressures on business trips and the costs of 'entertainment' are considerable barriers to wild living and, again contrary to the belief of some people, hotels are not populated with prostitutes and gigolos waiting for customers.

However, the temptations are there along with the dangers. Travellers have been known to yield to the temptation of sex and drugs especially in places where these are cheap. It is perhaps only necessary to remember that AIDS is a deadly disease and taking drugs (even the so-called soft variety) can be the start of a process which destroys the mental faculties and damages the body. Putting one's future and even one's life at risk in this way can be described quite simply: utterly stupid.

Summary

1. Business travel is not the free holiday some people imagine it to be and the demands made on the traveller can be heavy – both physically and mentally.

2. Loneliness, overeating, fatigue and alcohol can all weaken the defences and make the business traveller less effective and unwell.

3. Careful preparation is necessary and should include:

    - A realistic schedule with rest periods.
    - Taking a 'survival' kit for the treatment of minor ailments.
    - A check-up from the dentist.

4. Long-distance air travel can be exhausting and debilitating but a number of measures can be taken to reduce ill effects. There are a variety of 'remedies' for jet-lag, dehydration and other problems.

5. Choice of hotel, including location, is a factor in staying fit for business, e.g. a hotel with a fitness centre affords the opportunity for some therapeutic exercise. There are also ways to satisfy basic exercise needs if a swimming pool or other facility is not available.

6. Eating and drinking must be controlled, even if
    over-consumption is at times unavoidable. Special precautions
    must be taken in some countries to avoid tummy bugs.

7. Heatstroke and heat exhaustion can be problems in tropical
    countries, and, again, simple precautions should be taken.
    Precautions, in the form of appropriate clothing, should also be
    taken in very cold climates.

8. Avoid the temptations of the 'bright lights'.

PART 6

Getting Started and Following Through

31

Company action

THE BENEFITS of being Fit for Business described in Part 1 are sufficiently convincing, I hope, to prompt both companies and individuals to take some action. From the company point of view there are cash and commercial benefits to be gained from having healthy, energetic and switched-on employees, and investment in a company fitness programme can yield good returns. Let's consider first some of the things a company can do.

You, the reader, may be in a position to decide that your company will take action and what action it will be. Alternatively, while you may be convinced that the company should do something, it may be necessary to convert your colleagues to the idea. Experience suggests that capturing the interest of people in a new idea is not easily done with a general, vaguely attractive set of potential benefits – something very tangible is needed. That something is almost always money!

It will probably be necessary therefore to make some analysis of costs and potential savings and to produce a fitness profit and loss account. A good starting point can be the absenteeism records of the company and an analysis of the types of sickness absence recorded. Among the aspects to look for are:

- Percentage of days lost for sickness – and the cost.

- Reasons such as back pains, 'migraine', stomach upset and chills as compared with medically certificated illness. The minor ailments often fall under vague descriptions and result in absences of 1 or 2 days. These, as opposed to, say, hospital treatment for pneumonia, are capable of being reduced by means of a fitness campaign.

- The incidence of heart attacks or 'breakdowns'.

Using these data and costing out the apparent preventable absenteeism, you can provide figures to work out various scenarios, showing the wage and salary cost saving which would result from a 10 per cent reduction in time lost, a 20 per cent reduction, a 30 per cent reduction and so on. Against these savings can be set the capital cost of, say, a company fitness room equipped with a good range of exercise machines. The figures for savings quoted in Part 1 can be used, or some of the companies you know or believe to have in-house fitness facilities can be contacted for information. Help is also available from the British Heart Foundation, the Sports Council or the Health Education Authority. All these organisations can provide common-sense explanatory literature to support the case.

Another source of valuable evidence, and education, is to be found in the films produced by Millbank Films Limited, a subsidiary of ICI. Among films on health and safety available from Millbank are the following:

Better than cure – on occupational health.
One in Five – on heart attacks.
Mind your back – on lifting and posture.

A presentation of the facts and figures relating to your company combined with a convincing film may well be enough to overcome any complacency, apathy or lethargy that is preventing the company from taking action.

Alternatives available to the company

There are a number of actions which a health conscious company can take in addition to the in-house exercise facilities already mentioned. Here are some of them.

Regular health screening

A number of organisations, including the health insurance companies, provide routine screening. The advantage of this precaution lies in giving advance warning of a developing condition. Potentially serious diseases can be spotted at an early state, thus providing an opportunity to nip them in the bud. The advantages to the individual and the company are obvious.

A typical health screening scheme is the Well Woman Screening programme run by BUPA. This scheme includes tests on hearing, vision, lung function, blood pressure, blood analysis, cancer and so on. A similar scheme is provided for men.

Sending employees to health farms

A week at a health farm can put an unfit employee back on course, and the cost to the company is likely to be recouped in increased efficiency and higher productivity.

The health farm should be carefully chosen, as it is the nature of the programmes offered that is important, not the level of luxury provided. Facilities should include swimming pool, aerobics, exercise machinery and other supervised physical activity opportunities in addition to the usual saunas and spa baths. Most important of all in a health farm is a diagnostic service to work out the most appropriate programme to meet the needs of the individual. This service should be provided by professionally qualified medical staff, not just by a beautician or physical training instructor.

Some sterner stuff

The Outward Bound Trust provides a range of courses which are almost certain to improve physical fitness *and* improve self-confidence. There are courses suitable for the old and not so bold as well as for the young and adventurous, and all are run by experienced professionals.

It is likely that most people would be more attracted by a week in a comfortable health farm than a week scrambling about the Welsh hills and sleeping in a bunk. However, the Welsh hills may be the best choice for many individuals, and people who have completed Outward Bound courses speak enthusiastically about them. Do avoid a suggestion made by one senior executive – that senior staff should go to a health farm and juniors to Outward Bound! The health of the mind and body is far too important to be reduced to a matter of status symbols and the pathetic pomposity that lay behind the suggestion.

Paying for health club membership

An alternative for companies who are unable or unwilling to provide in-house facilities is to pay for an employee's membership of a health club. Payment could be in whole or part and dependent on regular attendance at the club.

Employing a fitness trainer

Larger companies might consider employing a resident professional to conduct exercise sessions, organise games and competitions, advise on diets etc. Qualifications suitable for this sort of job include BEd physical education, BA physical education, BSc sport and leisure studies or appropriate City & Guilds diplomas.

A helping hand and ear

Conventional thinking has it that the worker suffering from stress will find relief and consolation in the comforting bosom of the family. It has been assumed that the anxious, uptight executive will, at the end of a harrowing day, pour out his or her troubles to an understanding spouse and unwind in an atmosphere of domestic bliss and security. No doubt this happy scene is enacted in households round the globe, but what needs to be done if the stress comes not from the job but from the domestic environment itself? The effect of the stress in terms of sickness, poor quality work and irritability will be the same whatever its cause. The cost for the company will be just as great and, in a number of cases, has been measured in cash terms.

A leader in the task of dealing with stress caused by domestic factors is Control Data, an American computer company. In the 1970s Control Data set up a counselling and support service for employees with the initial objective of giving a helping hand in cases where drugs and drink had become a problem. Experience showed that help was also needed with other problems, including marriage breakdowns, which generated a great deal of stress in the people concerned. Control Data calculated that providing help to employees who had off-the-job problems saved the company about $10 million over a period of 10 years.

These results are supported by evidence provided by the Du Pont company, which reported substantial cash savings with a similar scheme, and General Motors, which recorded a 40 per cent drop in lost time and a remarkable 60 per cent fall in sickness and accident benefits. Analysis of the figures available suggests that in the USA, where counselling/ support services are more commonly found than in the UK, the net saving to the employer works out at between $25 and $33 per year per employee. There is now some interest being shown in dealing with off-the-job stress in the United Kingdom, where one company reported that it conservatively estimated the cost (to the company) of a divorce at £2,000.

There is therefore a convincing economic argument for setting up a support service to assist employees with the many and varied problems which can affect their health and so result in a low work performance. There is also a humanitarian argument but the evidence suggests that it is not necessary to rely on the altruism of the board to get a scheme off the ground. The problems which employees can face are many and varied and help may be needed for any of the following:

Marital breakdown	Alcoholism
Pension worries	Dependent relatives
Tax problems	Disasters, e.g. fire
House purchase	damage
Retirement planning	Drugs
Illness in the family	Death of the spouse
Job relocation	

The cost to a company of setting up a service to help with such problems will depend on the level of help provided. However, one company has estimated the cost as being between £15 and £25 per employee per year.

Some managers argue against such services on the grounds that domestic problems are not the business of the employer and that, in any case, employees are reluctant to make their problems known to the company. The fact that sickness, absenteeism and the like can result from domestic problems makes the subject very much the concern of the employer, unless he is content to see salary payments being wasted.

The problem of employees' reluctance to report their difficulties can be overcome by making the support services *entirely* independent from the rest of the management structure. Placing them, as appears reasonable at first sight, within the personnel department is a mistake. Employees will fear that, however confidential the service may be, there is a chance that their problems will be recorded and adversely influence promotion and salary prospects at a later date. It is not unknown for a manager to comment along the lines 'We can't recommend Snooks for this job. He has troubles at home and can't seem to sort them out'. If, instead, the service is operated quite separately and help is given entirely privately, employee reluctance to seek support will be much reduced.

Another argument made against such schemes is that many problems cannot be solved by a third party or at all. This is only partially true as illustrated by the following real-life case.

Harry was a good worker who had been with his company for about 15 years. He was not a high-flier but had a reputation for solid, dependable work and was popular with his colleagues. It was gradually noticed that he was becoming morose and unfriendly and also that his work had deteriorated. Harry, uncharacteristically, became unpunctual and started taking more and more odd days off for 'sickness'.

His boss took him to task for his poor quality work, with the result that Harry became even more 'difficult' and as time went on his performance became critical. Harry's boss, puzzled by the situation, asked a colleague from another department to interview him to see if he could get to the bottom of the problem. The interview produced some dramatic results. Harry broke down when asked the cause of his deterioration and explained that one of his children was dying of an incurable disease. He had lived with this agony for some months and both he and his wife were exhausted and seriously stressed.

There was nothing that the company could do to save

Harry's child but, once the problem was known, they could at least understand what was affecting him. In fact Harry's performance immediately began to improve because:

(a) He now knew that the employer knew – *and* was sympathetic and understanding.
(b) He had shared his problem and was relieved to find that the employer did not regard it as Harry's problem alone. Harry had not voluntarily mentioned the problem as he had expected the employer to adopt the view that his personal problems were not the company's concern.

Despite the fact that there was little the firm could do to tackle the basic problem, it did allow Harry time off when things were really bad and relieved him of some of the pressure in his job. They also reassured him that his job was safe.

In due course the child died, and with the passage of time Harry's work returned to normal. That was about 10 years ago and Harry is still there doing a good job. Without the counselling session he might well have ended up being dismissed from his job, and the company would have lost a good employee.

The sick building syndrome

There is now ample evidence to show that workers can suffer from illness caused by the building they work in. This sounds somewhat farfetched but the confirmed cases of legionnaire's disease (which can be fatal) have resulted in a great deal of attention being given to buildings in recent years. Fortunately most building-related illnesses are relatively minor and do not result in deaths; but they do cause absenteeism. The sick building syndrome, which includes headaches, dry skin and lethargy, is most commonly found in air-conditioned buildings and, in particular, those which are sealed to make them 'energy efficient'.

In such buildings the inhabitants are breathing recirculated air and all the bacteria which it contains. A confirmed case of this situation causing illness occurred in 1984 at an office in West London. After some dozens of people had become unwell (including some who collapsed), an investigation revealed that the air-conditioning system was the cause of the problem. Other cases have been reported by various experts, including a consultant physician at a Manchester hospital who, in addition to lethargy and headaches, includes nasal infections among the symptoms.

Another medical consultant has been reported as saying that the sick building syndrome may provide a scientific explanation of the Monday blues and that the cause is not limited to air conditioning. There is evidence that formaldehyde used in the manufacture of office carpets can cause nausea and headaches when it evaporates, and toxic chemicals can be produced by copying machines. Even fluorescent lighting can cause trouble: apparently the ultraviolet rays emitted can cause a smog of chemicals in the atmosphere that can result in eye complaints.

The sick building syndrome is currently receiving considerable attention in a number of countries (a government-funded research programme is being undertaken in the UK) but clearly the problem is not new. As long ago as 1969 a specialist office designer was asked to look at the layout of a large office building in Brussels. The people who worked there complained of headaches and drowsiness (especially in the afternoons) and, in some cases, nausea. The design specialist made the two following recommendations:

(i)   The air-conditioning system be changed to bring in new air as opposed to recirculated air.

(ii)   The layout be changed from a 'school room' style to a more varied style. He stated that the monotonous uniformity of the office and furniture was hypnotic.

Changing the layout was the easiest and quickest thing to do, and the result was a distinct reduction in the drowsiness problem. When the air circulation system was changed at a later date, the other symptoms also disappeared.

Bad chairs and bad backs

Sitting in a chair all day can be physically demanding. The classic example is the pain a typist can suffer in back, shoulders and neck when using an unsuitable chair. The same symptoms can occur in other occupations, with bad posture, enforced by poorly designed seating, resulting not only in pain but also in circulation problems and varicose veins.

Companies may find that some time and money spent on looking at their furniture will be well rewarded. Properly designed furniture is not necessarily more expensive than badly designed furniture, and productivity can be improved by using it.

32

Individual action

GETTING STARTED on a fitness campaign is often the most difficult stage for the individual. Somehow we must shake ourselves out of a comfortable rut and actually do something rather than just think about it. The difficulty can be added to by uncertainty about *what* to do and *why* to do it. The subject should be approached in a methodical way like any other business problem.

The first step is to identify the personal problems a fitness campaign might solve. Many of the possibilities have already been mentioned but now is the time to go through the following checklist:

1. Do you suffer from a stress problem?

   Some symptoms: Irritability.
   Indigestion.
   Insomnia.
   Headaches.

2. Do you have a fatigue problem?

   Some symptoms: Waking up feeling tired.
   Lack of energy for social/love life.
   No zest for life – can't be bothered.
   Persistent feeling of weariness.

3. Do you have a psychological problem?

   Some symptoms: Lack of confidence.
   Life seems pointless.

[187]

Job seems pointless.
Inferiority feelings.
Emotional problems.

4. Do you have a physical problem?

Some symptoms: Overweight.
Poor posture.
Shortness of breath.
Poor physical performance.

These are some of the problems, and, although listed above under separate headings, they are likely to be interdependent. In other words, feelings of inferiority, insomnia and lack of physical strength could all go together – as could other symptoms from the various categories.

The purpose of checking off the various symptoms is to identify the nature of your problem, if you have one – an essential prerequisite to doing something about it. The next step is to decide whether any of the symptoms are so serious that a medical check-up is needed. It could be the case that, say, persistent headaches, were caused by something other than stress and a lack of zest for life might be due to medical reasons rather than being the result of overwork and fatigue.

However, assuming there is nothing which requires the attention of the doctor, the construction of an action plan can be started. The first, and most essential stage, is to clearly define an objective. This is part of the 'planning cycle' which many business people will recognise as a technique often used to tackle problems in a methodical way. The technique can be illustrated diagrammatically:

```
                    SET OBJECTIVE
                                  ↘
REVISE _____ PREPARE PLAN
      ↖                                    ↙
        MONITOR PROGRESS ⟵_____ IMPLEMENT PLAN
```

It is particularly important that the objective be stated in as clear, positive and measurable a way as possible. Objectives such as 'To get fitter' or 'Feel better' are too vague, and it is difficult or impossible to measure achievement against them. The objective should be stated in such measurable terms as:

- To lose 10 lb in weight.

- To increase sleep from 4 to 6 hours a night.

- To recognise a point to life.

- To feel energetic enough to *want* to go to dinner parties.

Some of the objectives concerned with psychological problems will be difficult to define in measurable terms but every effort should be made to do so. If some definable and recognisable 'condition' can be described, it will provide a target to be aimed for and you will know when you have hit it.

Planning your fitness campaign

Having set the objective, you can work out a plan of action. The plan will first depend on the nature of the problem identified at an earlier stage and the objective(s) set. If, for instance, your objective is to lose weight and overcome feelings of inferiority, a two-pronged plan comprising a reduction in food intake and taking up a hobby may be needed. Fortunately the solution to one type of problem is likely to be the solution to another. Exercise, for example, will help with psychological as well as physical problems, and successful weight reduction is likely to result in improved self-confidence.

The plan will also need to take account of a number of other factors, including:

- The time that can be allocated for exercise, evening classes etc.

- Financial limitations.

- Personal likes and dislikes – although with some effort and determination some dislikes can be turned into sources of enjoyment.

Some very positive action will be necessary in order to overcome obstacles (such as lack of time) which may be at the very root of the problem in the first place. The workaholic will almost inevitably say that he or she has no time for playing games, taking up charity work or whatever. The whole fitness problem of the workaholic can be found in the fact that *all* available time is devoted to work. Breaking this mould will be difficult but it must be done if anything is to be achieved.

Personal preferences should be allowed for, providing they are not used as an excuse for doing nothing. If, for example, swimming is a favoured activity but there is no swimming pool conveniently available, some other activity must be chosen. The lack of a swimming pool should not be used as a reason to throw in the towel. (No pun intended!) However, there is no mileage to be gained in choosing something which is unattractive, as this will only become a discouragement to continuing with the campaign. One executive joined a fitness club *knowing* that the weight training provided by the club was something that bored him. Not surprisingly he abandoned his campaign, complaining that he did not enjoy it.

Boredom with a physical activity is a common problem, one that frequently causes people to give up. The underlying reason for this is that the person concerned, starting in an unfit condition, is obliged to grind away at the exercise in order to achieve any real degree of fitness. These early stages tend, as a result, to be rather tedious – whereas the later stages do not. A point will be reached where the physical achievement (distance covered, press-ups completed, machine exercise weights reached etc.) will in themselves become a source of satisfaction and interest. When, at a later stage still, sufficient fitness is gained to play squash or some other chosen game, then even more satisfaction and interest will result. It can, in fact, be helpful when constructing the plan to build in a series of stages designed to lead to more and more in the way of 'fun' elements and also to provide variety.

Other ways to make the early stages more acceptable and even interesting include:

- A week at a health farm to start the progamme.

- A physically demanding course such as Outward Bound.

- A monitored fitness course at a leisure centre.

A week at a health farm or at an Outward Bound centre can get you over the initial stages with the encouragement of trained instructors and other participants.

The same applies to monitored fitness courses, which are designed for the unfit executive who needs to get rid of a flabby body and relieve a threatened heart. These courses start with a thorough medical examination and continue with graduated training sessions which will take the individual *safely* from an unfit condition to being capable of sustained physical activity.

The whole thing is made easier by the presence of other participants – all of whom will have a similar problem. Sharing the sweat and toil often develops a friendly rivalry, adding interest, and often a camaraderie, which leads to a light-hearted atmosphere. Participants soon discover the mental and physical pleasures of a post-session sense of achievement and relaxation. A long, hot shower followed by a cool drink in the bar (and the inevitable banter and leg-pulling) round off each session very pleasantly. Allowance is made for age, and the older executive need not be put off by the fear of being expected to do too much. There is normally, in any group, a range of ages, and the possession of a head of grey hair (or none at all) does not mean that anyone is likely to feel out of place.

Finally, don't forget to provide, in your plan, for year-round activity. Indoor sports in the winter can be matched with summer activities, whilst evening classes can be found almost throughout the whole year. If an allotment is chosen as a form of recreation, this too will provide almost all-year-round activity – tidying up can be done even when the ground is frozen hard.

Typical objectives and plan

The following plan is offered as a 'model' for what may be done. Your own plan will of course be tailored to your own objectives, which, in turn, will be tailored to your own problems. However, no harm is likely to be done and much gained if, uncertain of what to do, you follow this plan.

Objectives

(i)   To reduce weight until nothing wobbles during the 'mirror test'. Estimated amount to be reduced – 10 lb.

(ii) To achieve enough physical fitness to be able to recommence playing tennis at club level.

(iii) To find a source of self-fulfilment outside work and to develop it until the dissatisfactions with the job are no longer a source of anxiety.

Plan

Stage 1. Visit doctor for a check-up to ensure that no basic problems exist.

Timing – earliest possible appointment.

Stage 2. Commence following changes to diet:

- No sugar in tea or coffee.

- Cut out sugary food, e.g. cakes.

- Reduce alcohol consumption by 50 per cent.

- Reduce fat intake by 50 per cent and switch to polyunsaturated only.

- Generally reduce portions if you are overweight.

Timing – immediate.

Stage 3. (a) List all the non-work subjects of interest which you could develop as an absorbing hobby.
(b) Research local evening-class opportunities.
(c) Research local leisure centre and similar facilities to find opportunities for exercise.

Timing – to be completed in 10 days.

Stage 4. Commence chosen exercise course.
Commence evening classes.

Timing – earliest possible enrolment.

Implementation

The biggest obstacle to implementation is taking too much time in making up your mind what to do. It is for this reason that the stages of the plan should have some time limits applied to them. In other words, the search for a suitable evening class or whatever should start immediately and should be completed within a definite period of time. It may be useful also to stipulate a deadline for deciding on which class or course to choose, even if the start dates of these activities are some time ahead.

Whatever the circumstances, a limit should be set to researching the possibilities, as this process can go on for months. The same thinking should be applied to choosing something, i.e. the absolutely ideal requirement may not be immediately or readily available so a near substitute should be chosen to ensure that something is done.

Monitoring

Keeping a check on progress serves three purposes. Firstly, it will provide a means to see that something is being done and, secondly, it will provide encouragement. Thirdly, if the wrong choice has been made and the programme is clearly not providing progress towards an objective, the monitoring will reveal this sad fact. Once it is seen to be faulty, the plan can be revised accordingly. Encouragement will be gained from seeing the results of all the effort being made.

The choice of monitoring systems is important. Whatever method is used must mean something. Fortunately many of them are objective rather than subjective in nature and 'measurements' will be easy. The easy ones include such things as:

- Weight loss.

- Time to jog one mile.

- Number of lengths swum.

- Miles cycled in one hour.

The more subjective measures are largely those concerned with the psychological objectives, which may amount to feeling more at peace with the world. Whether or not such objectives have been achieved will depend on the individual's perception of his or her own behaviour and feelings. However, some numerical comparison may be possible and the individual will usually know whether or not progress is being made. Apart from less frequent or shorter periods of anxiety or similarly unwelcome mental states, the following can be a guide:

- Reduced frequency of rows with colleagues or spouse.

- Reduction in the number of times that a stiff drink is felt to be essential for survival.

- Increased hours of uninterrupted sleep.

Otherwise success can be exemplified by finding work more interesting, problems less oppressive and colleagues seeming to be more reasonable.

One executive, well known for his bad temper and 'difficult' personality, had, for a long time, been overworked and was showing severe signs of stress. His company sent him on a sabbatical to carry out some research on a relatively undemanding topic and he returned much refreshed. A couple of weeks after his return he was heard to remark how much some of his close colleagues had changed during his absence. 'They are much more reasonable', he said 'I don't know what has changed them but whatever it was it's now much easier to work in this place!'

On a purely physical level, one standard test of progress which is widely used is the recovery time check. The person concerned records his or her pulse rate when fully rested. A period of exercise is then carried out and the pulse rate measured again. The pulse is then checked repeatedly until the rate has returned to normal (i.e. where it started). The *time* required for the rate to return to normal is a measure of fitness. The shorter the time, the fitter you are. It is likely that as time goes on it will be noticed that the pulse rate when you are resting has also decreased. This is another sign of fitness – at least in so far that the heart does not have to work so hard to give the body the oxygen and nutrients that are needed. Repeating precisely the same period of exercise at regular intervals and checking the recovery time gives a good indication of progress and provides a source of interest in a fitness campaign.

In monitored fitness courses there are likely to be built-in progress checks. Alternatively, you can develop your own simple measuring methods in addition to the recovery time system described above. One easy way is to choose a series of exercises, say – sit-ups, press-ups, jumps, dumb-bell lifts, and squat thrusts – and go through each of them in turn for exactly 30 seconds each. Counting the number completed in 30 seconds provides a measure of progress when compared with previous results.

Revising your plan

If things are not going well, it may be necessary to revise your plan. A change of direction, if decided on for good reason, is not an admission of defeat but rather a realistic and sensible reaction. It may be found, for example, that losing weight by eating less is providing particularly diffi-cult. In such a case it may be easier or more practicable to lose the unwanted pounds by changing your diet or step-ping up the exercise programme. Many people find that exercise is a lot more enjoyable than struggling with a diet and the other benefits of a stronger, more efficient body will be gained at the same time.

The calorie values of various forms of exercise are, unfortunately, variously stated by different experts, but if one works on the basis that 30 minutes' fairly brisk walking is equivalent to about 180 calories, then some estimate of one's own can be made. An equivalent time on the squash or tennis court should burn up about twice as much, providing the games are vigorous and include some good rallies. A steady swimming session of 30 minutes is likely to burn off something over 200 calories, depending on the stroke used.

The calorie consumption of exercise depends to some extent on the weight of the individual as well as the nature of the work done. Whatever the weight loss achieved may be, many people will find the exercise method more enjoyable than the dieting method.

Revision of the plan may also be necessary if too tough a target was chosen. If you find that you are overdoing it and achieving the chosen objective is becoming a wearisome chore, then slow down. In relation to exercise keep in mind these rules (some of which have been mentioned before):

- Set goals but be sure they are realistic.

- Train as hard as you can but don't strain.

- Don't over-train – this can cause fatigue and injury.

- Warm up before the work-out.

- Vary your programme to make it interesting.

- Train at regular intervals – not spasmodically.

You may have chosen a form of solitary exercise and find yourself feeling lonely. If so, join a club or find a companion to exercise with you. Sharing the effort with someone else is likely to make it more enjoyable and stimulating.

Don't hesitate to change direction either if you are

attending evening classes or developing a hobby. Having given your first choice *a good try* and not finding it to your liking, you will find little point in going on. It is better to start again than to persist with something unappealing or which provides little or no enjoyment. Continuing may create the very stress you are trying to get rid of.

Following through

The people who run fitness courses, managers of leisure centres and the like often remark how frequently achievement is not followed through. Thoroughly unfit people will work hard at, say, a monitored fitness course, reach a good standard of fitness – and then give up. Six months later these people have returned to their former overweight, stressed condition.

To avoid this regression and the waste of time and effort, a positive 'follow through' plan is needed. To some extent this means a permanent change in life-style, which can include one or more of the following:

- Joining, say, a badminton club, so that you continue exercising on a regular basis. If the badminton is combined with a weekly (and regular) swim, jog, walk or whatever appeals to you, so much the better.

- Maintaining the change of diet in the form of smaller quantities, less animal fat, lower sugar intake – or whatever was used to achieve the original objective.

- Permanently maintaining a reduced alcohol intake – perhaps more tonic and less gin or all tonic and *no* gin.

- Keeping to the same working hours as adopted during the campaign, e.g. keeping weekends entirely free for recreation.

- Choosing a new evening class to follow the last one, e.g. by moving from the beginners' level to the intermediate and then to an advanced class.

- Taking a regular annual week with Outward Bound or a similar demanding course. This will act as a jolt to a system which may be slowing down or to a fall-off in your determination and enthusiasm.

- Looking for a new way to obtain self-fulfilment every year or two. The water-colour painting may be going well but perhaps learning calligraphy or photography will add a further sense of purpose to life.

- If you are an over-stressed workaholic, learning how to delegate *and practising it*. This will not only make your life better but will also give your subordinates more interest in their jobs too, providing the delegation is carried out properly. There are many books on delegating for those who have doubts as to how to go about it.

- Checking yourself methodically every 6 months to see whether you are slipping back into your old ways, putting on surplus weight, or feeling anxious and stressed again. If the regression is slight, a minor adjustment to life-style may be enough to do the trick. If severe, the regression may require starting all over again with objectives, plan and implementation. Alternatively, a short, sharp shock in the form of a week on a suitable course may pull things round.

Summary

1. Companies can get started by assessing the cash value of a fitness campaign for their staff. The pay-off can be attractive in reduced absenteeism and less wasted money.

2. A number of organisations such as the British Heart Foundation can give advice to companies who are uncertain of the likely benefits or don't know how to proceed.

3. A range of options is available to companies, from health screening to providing counselling and support services to employees.

4. The sick building syndrome is something for companies to take seriously and the working environment can be checked out – with a potential for profit.

5. Action by individuals should be methodically worked out, starting with an analysis of the problems. Having decided what the problems are, the individual can set objectives, devise a plan and implement it. Of course, you may not have any problems but the same action can be taken to create new interests or to become healthier.

6. The progress of the plan must be monitored and, if necessary, revised. Once the objective(s) has been achieved, it is important to follow through to prevent a return to the original problems – and waste of the effort put in.

PART 7

APPENDICES

More Information and Sources of Even More

Appendix 1

More about Maslow's Hierarchy Theory

ABRAHAM MASLOW, an American researcher, published a theory of human motivation which is simple and convincing. The theory, like many ideas, is one of those things which are obvious once pointed out.

Maslow put forward the view that people are motivated by various needs which start with the obvious bodily ones and ascend through a hierarchy to self-fulfilment needs. He classified the needs into the following five groups:

1. Bodily needs — To satisfy hunger, thirst, sleep.

2. Safety needs — A sense of security and protection from danger.

3. Social needs — Social activity, love and a feeling of belonging.

4. Self-esteem needs — Status and the respect of other people.

5. Self-fulfilment needs – Accomplishment, creativity and 'personal growth'.

Maslow pointed out that until the lower needs are met the higher needs are ignored. In other words, a starving person is not much concerned with safety or social activity – until food has been obtained.

Since executives are normally well fed and watered, it is the social and other needs which require to be satisfied, and Maslow argues that any failure to do so can result in frustration. This in turn can lead to aggressive attitudes, non-cooperation and a sense of apathy. This unhappy mental condition can develop into mental illness – particularly if Maslow's level 5 requirements are not satisfied. To be mentally fit for business and well motivated, the job and its environment should provide the means to satisfy the higher level needs. If it does not, the individual may have to create his or her own opportunities *outside* the job.

A number of other researchers have drawn attention to the need for self-esteem and a sense of fulfilment to be provided by a job – and the demotivating effects of their absence. Frederick Hertzberg drew attention to these needs, using different terms to describe them, in his book *The Motivation to Work*, written jointly with B. Mausner and B. B. Snydeman in 1959. More ideas on the subject were provided by Hertzberg in *Work and the Nature of Man*, published by Staples Press in 1968. Hertzberg and his colleagues refer to 'Achievement' and 'Growth' as important factors, and also point out that elements in a worker's *personal* life are influential in his or her work performance.

A good book covering the theories of some twenty researchers is *Developments in Management Thought* by Harold R. Pollard, published by Heinemann in 1974 and reprinted in 1978; it may be difficult to find, but a browse around the second-hand bookshops could be time well spent for executives who want to learn more.

Although the ideas included in this book have been around for a long time, they are none the worse for that. Human nature has not noticeably changed in the last 30 years and something which made someone more or less fit for business in the 1950s will equally well apply in the decades to come.

Appendix 2

More on aromatherapy

The evidence in favour of aromatherapy as a cure for mental and physical ailments is virtually entirely empirical. Very little scientific research has been made into the subject and acceptance of aromatherapy as a genuine form of therapy is based on the reactions of patients. However, work done by Russian and French scientists has shown that various essential oils will destroy certain bacteria and also that when rubbed into the skin of a guinea pig the oils are absorbed into the bloodstream and carried to various internal organs. No one seems to know whether this happens in human beings or whether, if it does, the result is beneficial or otherwise.

However, based on the largely empirical evidence, aromatherapists maintain that the treatment promotes healing, encourages the growth of new cells, aids the reduction of scar tissue and relieves stress. The growing popularity of aromatherapy and the increasing number of 'satisfied customers' suggests that it is well worth serious consideration if only as a pick-me-up for the tired executive.

The following is a more comprehensive list of the plant oils used and the conditions they are used for:

Basil   – Antiseptic and to treat insomnia.

Bergamot   – Antiseptic and to 'calm the nerves'.

Cinnamon   – Antiseptic and for treating scabies.

Cloves   – An analgesic (an old dental treatment).

Eucalyptus – For conditions affecting the nasal and bronchial passages.

Geranium – For stimulating the circulation.

Jasmine – Sedative and to increase skin elasticity.

Lavender – Antiseptic, diuretic, anti-rheumatic and to treat wounds and burns.

Lemongrass – Treats acne and 'helps to improve energy'.

Marjoram – Nervous stress and rheumatic conditions.

Peppermint – Decongestant and also for treating sunburn.

Sage – Antiseptic and for over-exercised muscles and general aches and pains.

Thyme – Dermatitis.

Ylang-ylang – Antiseptic and for impotence and frigidity!

Recommended further reading on the subject comprises *Aromatherapy for the whole person*, by Dr W. E. Arnould-Taylor, and published by Stanley Thornes (Publishers) Ltd; and *Aromatherapy Handbook*, by Daniele Ryman, and published by Century.

Appendix 3

Herbs

Enthusiasts for herbs claim that, in addition to their value as flavourings, many have curative and health-giving values.

Herbs have been used for centuries as medicines and as long ago as the fourteenth century purslane was said to 'mytygate great heat in all in the inward parts of man'. Purslane in those days was used as a cure for lasciviousness! The interesting thing is that purslane has been found to contain substantial quantities of omega-3 fatty acids. Other recent research, including work done at Edinburgh University, indicates that lack of fatty acids can encourage heart disease. This is a variation on the idea that too much fat encourages heart disease. The implications now are that it is a diet lacking polyunsaturated fat (which contains fatty acids) which causes the trouble, and it is the saturated animal fats, which do not provide fatty acids, which should be avoided.

Since purslane can be a source of fatty acids, it may be good for the heart – whatever its effect may be on lasciviousness. William Cobbett, writing in 1829, naturally had no knowledge of the fatty acid aspect of purslane. If he had, he might not have said of it 'A mischievous weed eaten by Frenchmen and pigs when they can get nothing else'.

Herbs should not be dismissed as a quaint hangover from the past. Many have been shown to have beneficial properties – even stinging nettles are rich in minerals and vitamin C.

The following are some of the curative properties claimed:

Dill   – a treatment for upset stomach.

Hyssop – for coughs and sore throats.

Rue   – as a relief from indigestion.

Violet   – for the relief of headaches.

Sceptics should keep in mind that for many years foxglove tea was used as a treatment for heart disease. In modern times foxglove was found to contain digitalin, an alkaloid which can be effective in treating certain conditions. There could well be genuine value in other herbs – if nothing else but to enhance the flavour of food.

Appendix 4

Sex life and fitness

Monks, nuns and other celibate people show no obvious signs that the absence of sex in their lives affects their health one way or another. However, recent medical research strongly suggests that there is a link between sex life and health – at least in respect to women.

Dr Winnifred Cutler, a specialist in behavioural endocrinology at the Pennsylvania School of Medicine, has carried out research into the role that sexual activity plays in the health of women. Dr Cutler has been reported as saying that 'men are really important to women' – in the sense that regular heterosexual activity is beneficial. Among the benefits claimed are:

- Normal menstrual cycles.

- Fewer infertility problems.

- Fewer menopausal problems.

Dr Cutler has produced evidence to show that the male scent (pheromones) can alter the timing of the menstrual cycle, and other researchers have concluded that pheromones improve the 'physiological functioning' of women. Since there is some evidence that the health of a woman's reproductive system is a pointer to her general health, then there is a potential link between sex life and fitness – at least in the case of women. Dr Cutler has been reported as concluding that 'for most women regular sex with a man would seem to be an important part of good health'.

The pheromones which appear to play such a vital part in this sex life-health cycle do not, it seems, affect women at a distance. Intimate contact is required and working in an office surrounded by men is said to have no effect at all.

There is, in addition, evidence that kisses and cuddles can have beneficial results. These benefits, possibly more psychological than physical, indicate that the degree of intimate contact required need not necessarily include intercourse. Dr Vernon Coleman, writing in a magazine in September 1986, stated that a kiss and a cuddle rather than the traditional apple will keep the doctor away. Whether or not the important pheromones are transmitted during the course of a kiss or cuddle is not clear but an American insurance company has revealed some interesting information. Apparently it claims that if a woman kisses a man goodbye every morning, his life expectancy improves. An average of 5 years more life is claimed!

On the debit side there is a recently expounded theory that being 'in love' can be bad for the executive. According to an article in the *Independent*, aptly published on St Valentine's day 1987, people in love produce a lot of endorphines. These substances, mentioned in Part 2, which are those released during exercise, can create a sense of euphoria. The article suggests that the increased endorphine makes people behave uncharacteristically and reminds the reader of Freud's view that being in love is a form of madness. Apart from looking healthy, people in love are prone to irrational decision-taking, which could be disastrous in the business environment.

Also on the debit side is what has been termed the 'Fiancée Factor'. Two doctors in the USA have recorded cases where heart patients have died shortly after visits (successively) from their wives and their mistresses. The *Journal of the American Medical Association* has pointed out that emotional stress can trigger off heart attacks and there is ample anecdotal evidence that illicit affairs can cause health problems. The irony is that in its early stages an affair can be stimulating (endorphine again?) but once the relationship becomes serious, trouble can start. Dealing with the conflicting demands of spouse and lover and living with guilt feelings can be extremely stressful.

If aphids are anything to go by, pheromones could have a lot to answer for. Research carried out at Rothamsted Research Station has shown that the female aphid uses pheromones to lure the male. According to a researcher at Rothamsted, 'the female aphid waves its legs around to spread the pheromone and attract males'. Presumably the male aphid finds this performance irresistible, and aphid behaviour may give us a clue to the cause of some of the less rational human behaviour!

Appendix 5

Redundancy sickness

Redundancy has been a more or less constant threat in recent years to many executives, and the effects on the individual have been well publicised. There is a significant danger that the health of the redundant person will suffer as a result of the loss of a job at the very time that fitness for business is most needed. The unemployed executive needs to be in a fit state both mentally and physically to tackle the problem and fight his or her way back.

The capability must be there to calmly and methodically set about obtaining another job or setting up in business on one's own. Doing this requires determination, courage, persistence and cunning – all of which are likely to be in short supply in the person suffering the potentially shattering effects of being kicked out. Fortunately there are solutions to this problem.

The various ill-effects of redundancy reported by its victims can be summarised as follows:

- A loss of 'self-identity'.
- Anxiety or depression.
- Inferiority feelings.
- A feeling of loneliness.

Some redundant people have described their feelings as similar to those experienced after a bereavement, and most describe this reaction as changing with the passage of time.

Generally time is *not* a healer in redundancy cases. After the initial shock comes apathy and a sense of hopelessness, which may worsen as the months go by with no sign of another job – all of which is a reminder of Maslow's theory.

These reactions and feelings are not dissimilar to those of the executive who has been passed over for promotion or whose job provides lots of frustrations and no satisfaction. Stress looms large as a possibility, as does the ill-health which can follow a long period of stress.

The solution lies in all the recommended exercises and sources of self-fulfilment which have already been described – combined with a very positive attitude. The redundant person may find some help from friends, relatives or even consultants specialising in this field, but basically the solution must be self-created. One senior executive who suddenly found himself on the street spent his first week sitting at a table planning his future. He made a positive decision to treat his unemployment problem like the many business problems he had dealt with, by analysis and planning. It helps to write down one's objectives, write down steps to be taken (e.g. listing people to be contacted) and generally planning an aggressive campaign.

This approach can be backed up by exercise to raise the spirits and boost confidence, classes and courses to learn new skills and any social activity which provides psychological support. All the possibilities should be listed and explored, including self-employment. There are many opportunities for working from home as a self-employed person despite initial appearances to the contrary.

The *Daily Mail Guide to Working from Home* lists some of the possibilities and gives some practical ideas on how to go about investigating and exploiting them.

If throughout it all the redundant executive keeps up regular physical exercise, both body and mind will be better equipped to deal with a serious and potentially devastating situation.

Appendix 6

Signs of disease

In all cases of persistent pain or other worrying symptoms medical advice should be sought. Busy executives tend to put this off until too late, so, with no apology for a degree of brutality, the following are the warning signs of five killer diseases.

  (i) *Heart attack or angina*

A crushing vice-like pain in the chest, often brought on by physical exertion, excitement or unwelcome news.

 (ii) *Strokes*

Mini-strokes lasting a few hours produce disturbed vision, weakness on one side of the body and speech impairment. One or more mini-strokes may occur before 'the big one' comes along.

(iii) *Lung cancer*

Nagging cough which will not go away, spitting blood-stained mucus and shortness of breath. Weight loss may also be an early symptom.

(iv) *Breast cancer*

Persistent lumps in the breast, swelling in the upper arm and/or one breast becoming larger than the other. The skin of the breast may become puckered and the nipple turn inwards.

(v)   *Cervical cancer*

Bleeding (other than menstrual) from the vagina and/or a discharge. Intercourse will probably be painful.

If any of these symptoms appear a doctor should be consulted. The chances are that, despite one or two symptoms, there is in fact nothing seriously wrong; or the trouble can be discovered at an early stage and then dealt with.

For further, qualified, information and advice the following organisations can help:

Coronary Prevention Group,
60 Great Ormond Street,
London, WC1 3HR

Chest, Heart and Stroke Association,
Tavistock House North,
Tavistock Square,
London, WC1H 9JE

Women's National Cancer Control Campaign,
1 South Audley Street,
London, W1Y 5DQ

Appendix 7

Winter depression

Almost everyone becomes more and more fed up as the winter months go by. Tempers tend to be shorter when the days are shorter and the incidence of coughs, colds and influenza is higher. For most people the winter months result in more frequent and longer periods of being 'fed up' – a condition which rapidly fades when spring arrives or which can be cured by a relaxing weekend break.

For others the problem is more serious, and a marked inability to work effectively (or at all) can develop. This is a situation which has only recently been fully recognised, and doctors have given it the name Seasonal Affected Disorder or SAD. The first recorded description of SAD was provided by a German psychologist early in the century but nothing much in the way of research was done until the 1980s. The recent investigations have shown that the problem is very real and is caused by a lack of sunlight.

The classic symptoms are those of people who have an urge to opt out. Such people will resign their jobs, lose interest in social activities and generally go into a form of 'mental hibernation'. Less serious cases exhibit a general lethargy, loss of efficiency and inability to concentrate.

The number of people affected by real SAD is likely to be a good deal less than 5 per cent but if it is only, say, 1 per cent, then every company of any size is likely to have one or two sufferers.

Research is focused on the use of special types of light as a cure. There is evidence that the symptoms can be entirely removed in some people by a daily exposure to certain wavelengths. It is also interesting to note that research at Harvard Medical School has provided evidence that the symptoms of jet-lag (insomnia and fatigue) can also be cured by light therapy. The current hypothesis is that crossing time zones, in such a way as to reduce the period of experienced daylight, has a similar effect to the short winter days.

An awareness that SAD is a real and not imagined condition at least enables us to allow for it in ourselves and others. SAD may be the reason why Mr A and Mrs B are performing badly at their jobs.

Appendix 8

Irradiated food – good or bad?

At the time of writing, food irradiation is illegal in Britain although permitted in a number of countries. Recommendations have been made to the government by a committee of scientists that Britain too should legalise irradiation. The argument in favour of this process amounts to a reduction in the incidence of food poisoning. Irradiation, it is argued, will kill off the bacteria which contribute to the yearly 15,000 or so reported cases of food poisoning. It has been pointed out by Professor Alan Holmes of the Leatherhead Food Research Association that irradiation does not make the food radioactive and does not harm the food itself.

Opponents of the idea claim that irradiation can destroy some vitamins and, once the process is completed, it is difficult to tell if it has been done properly. However, the advising committee believes the risks to be small and no more than with existing heat treatments.

No doubt the politicians will decide and may leave the unwilling consumer with no choice but to grow his own or starve. All the more reason to start an allotment!

Appendix 9

Where to go to get fit

Sports and leisure centres

There are over 1,000 indoor centres available, in addition to the many private clubs. A complete guide giving all the locations can be obtained from your local regional office of the Sports Council or from its head office at 16 Upper Woburn Place, London, WC1H 0QP. Telephone No. 01–388 1277.

The Sports Council also publishes a magazine, *Sport and Leisure*, which gives information on a wide range of topics, including sporting events and opportunities.

Health farms

The following is a selection to consider. It is advisable to obtain a brochure from those which interest you to check that both price and the treatments available suit your requirements.

CEDAR FALLS HEALTH FARM, Taunton, Somerset. Tel. 0823–433233.

CHAMPNEYS, Tring, Hertfordshire. Tel. 04427–3351.

FOREST MERE, Liphook, Hampshire. Tel. 0428–722051.

GRAYSHOTT HALL, Hindhead, Surrey. Tel. 042873–4331.

HENLOW GRANGE, Henlow, Bedfordshire. Tel. 0462–811111.

INGLEWOOD HEALTH HYDRO, Reading, Berkshire.
Tel. 0488–82022.

RAGDALE HALL, Melton Mowbray, Leicestershire. Tel.
06647–5831.

SHRUBLAND HALL, Coddenham, Suffolk. Tel. 0473–
830404.

TYRINGHAM CLINIC, Newport Pagnell,
Buckinghamshire. Tel. 0908–610450.

Smokers and drinkers should take note that some of these
places may ban tobacco and alcohol, so be sure you can
'take it' before booking.

The great outdoors

The Outward Bound Trust runs courses at Lock Eil, Ulls-
water, Eskdale, Rhownier and Aberdovey.

Activities include rock climbing, abseiling, sailing,
canoeing and orienteering. All the courses are run by
experienced instructors and all specialist clothing and
equipment is provided. The instructors give maximum
support to participants, who are encouraged to discover
just how far they can go. This is often much further than
first thought, resulting in a welcome boost to confidence
and self-esteem.

Details of courses are available from:

Outward Bound Trust,
Chestnut Field,
Regent Place,
Rugby, CV21 2PJ

The National Centre for Mountain Activities offers a range
of courses at Betws-y-Coed in North Wales. The courses
include an introduction to rock climbing, big wall climbing,

scrambles in Snowdonia, hill walking, orienteering, canoeing and much more to develop the body and the confidence.

Participants need to be in fairly good shape before arriving, as most of the courses are physically demanding. Like Outward Bound, the NCMA provides experienced instructors and all the specialist equipment.

Courses can also be specially tailored to the needs of groups, which are offered special rates. This may be attractive to companies that wish to send a number of employees together on a course.

Full details and a brochure can be obtained from:

National Centre for Mountain Activities,
Capel Curig,
Betws-y-Coed,
Gwynedd
Tel. 06904–214

Hang-gliding, water skiing, surfing and sailing are available at Carnkie Farm House, Redruth, Cornwall and walking holidays in Wales are organised by High Trek Snowdonia (Tel. 0286–871232). Other outdoor activity breaks can be found in the English Tourist Board's Activity Holiday Guide.

Dancing

An enjoyable way to improve fitness, dancing also has a pleasant social side. Your yellow pages can give you details of dancing schools in your area. For people in or near London the Contemporary Dance School offers courses, including ballet and jazz dancing. It also provides body conditioning. Details can be obtained on Tel. No. 01–387 0152.

Appendix 10

Fitness testing and health screening

Details of the BUPA scheme for health screening (mentioned in Part 2) can be obtained from BUPA Medical Centre London, Battle Bridge House, 300 Gray's Inn Road, London, WC1X 8DV.

There are other screening services available and it is a good idea to compare costs and the scope of the tests. Possible alternatives are the Cromwell Hospital, Cromwell Road, London, SW5 0TU; and Medical Express, Chapel Place, Oxford Street, London, W1.

Instead of, or perhaps additional to, the do-it-yourself fitness testing already described, you may wish to use a professional service. Employers intending to use fitness testing as part of an in-house campaign will probably prefer more scientific methods.

Many of the organisations offering fitness tests will also provide monitored programmes to improve fitness. One such is AMI Health Care Ltd, 4 Cornwall Terrace, London, NW1 4QP. This organisation operates from twelve locations in England and Scotland – enquirers should ask for details of their Lifestyle Programme.

Fitness tests form part of a 10-week programme run by The Fitness Centre at the West London Institute of Higher Education, Lancaster House Campus, Borough Road, Isleworth, Middlesex; and comprehensive testing is carried out by SAFA, Gardens Health Club, 27 Kingly Street, London, W1. SAFA is run by a team of doctors who use computer-linked equipment to obtain a detailed picture of the subject's fitness.

A good fitness test will report on your heart and lung efficiency, fat:muscle ratios and oxygen consumption. Such tests are also available at some of the larger leisure centres, often as a preliminary to monitored get-fit courses.

Appendix 11

Vaccinations and inoculations

The following are some of the countries for which a valid certificate of vaccination against yellow fever is required. Those marked with (R) are countries for which a cholera inoculation is recommended.

Angola (R)	Ghana (R)	Nigeria (R)
Benin (R)	Guinea-Bissau (R)	Panama
Bolivia	Guinea Republic	Senegal (R)
Cameroon (R)	(R)	Somalia (R)
Chad (R)	Ivory Coast (R)	Togo (R)
Congo (R)	Liberia (R)	Uganda (R)
Ethiopia (R)	Mali (R)	Zambia (R)

It should be noted that some countries, not listed above, will require certificates if the traveller has travelled from countries where cholera or yellow fever are endemic. Regulations change from time to time, and if in doubt check with the appropriate embassy.

A jab against typhoid is desirable before visiting certain countries and this precaution should be taken in respect of a stay in any country in tropical Africa, plus:

Algeria	Ethiopia	Papua New
Bangladesh	Indonesia	Guinea
Bolivia	Korea	Sri Lanka
Burma	Nepal	Thailand
		Yemen (N. and S.)

The authorities change their requirements and recommendations from time to time; if in any doubt at all, it is wise to err on the safe side and check with a doctor.

Appendix 12

Further reading

In addition to publications already mentioned, the following will be found to be helpful.

Exercise

Exercise, Health and Medicine – available from the publications department of the Sports Council. The contents are devoted to the proceedings of the 1984 international conference at Lilleshall on the proven medical benefits of exercise.

A good book on the treatment of back pain by the use of exercise is *Back in Action*, by Sarah Key, published by Bantam.

Dr Kenneth Cooper (whose work was mentioned in Part 2) is the author of *Running Without Fear*, published by Pathway. In this book Dr Cooper emphasises the aerobic types of exercise and recommends what to choose, how much to do and how often. Dr Cooper, by the way, is said to be the man who invented the word 'aerobics'.

Some basic commonsense advice is available in 'Looking After Yourself', a Health Education Council booklet. This publication gives all the basic information needed in about 10 pages.

Food and drink

A book which argues in favour of a good breakfast, i.e.

more than the black coffee and orange juice variety, is *Brain Food*, by Brian and Roberta Morgan, published by Michael Joseph. The authors believe that without a good breakfast office workers will be less efficient by mid-morning, and they offer dietary advice to deal with insomnia, poor memory and hangovers.

Some dire warnings about alcohol are given in a report entitled *Alcohol, Our Favourite Drug*, available from Tavistock Publications; and the Health Education Authority booklet 'That's the Limit' offers some readable advice. A self-help guide to anyone seeking ways to cut alcohol intake is provided in *Let's Drink to Your Health*, by Robertson and Heather (British Psychological Society).

The diet debate is examined in *A Diet of Reason: Sense and Nonsense in the Healthy Eating Debate* edited by Digby Anderson and published by the Social Affairs Unit. Less heavy going is 'Food for Thought', available from the Health Education Authority – as is 'Looking After Yourself' (mentioned under exercise) which gives four pages of simple advice on food and fitness.

Additives are dealt with in 'Food Additives in Perspective', which can be obtained from the Food Policy Research Unit, School of Biomedical Studies, Bradford University, Bradford BD7 1DP.

The 'dieting makes you fat' theory briefly described in Part 3 is fully covered in *Dieting Makes you Fat*, by Cannon and Einzig, published by Sphere. This book is an interesting read.

A good all-round book on what to eat is *Nutritional Medicine, the Drug-free Guide to Better Family Health*. This book, published by Pan, is written by Dr Stephen Davies and Dr Alan Stewart, who challenge some of the traditional views of the medical profession.

Miscellaneous

Problems with the feet can be debilitating, inconvenient and embarrassing even if not painful. The executive who has a lot of travelling to do needs healthy feet, as does anyone whose job includes lots of standing or walking. The problems can vary from flat feet, fungal infection, and ingrowing toenails to smelly feet! A book dealing with such problems is *Have Healthy Feet*, by Lyn Carter, published by Javelin Books.

A book which concentrates on the problems of waking up feeling washed out and general exhaustion is *How to Fight Fatigue*, by Louis Proto (Century).

A useful book that helps executives and managers to identify and deal with stress in others within their organisation is Dr Vernon Coleman's *Stress Management Techniques*, published by Mercury Books (W.H. Allen). Also published by Mercury Books is Geoffrey Whitehead's *An Office in Every Home*, a complete guide to all aspects, including psychological, of working from home.

Suggestions for dealing with pre-menstrual tension are provided in a booklet entitled 'The Practitioners Guide to PMS', which can be obtain from the Pre-Menstrual Tension Advisory Service, PO Box 268, Hove, Sussex, BN3 1RW. The booklet offers advice on coping with the stress which might be the cause of the problem and also suggests dietary remedies. The PMTAS estimates that as many as 73 per cent of women suffer from this problem, which the service believes is under-diagnosed.

The Vogue Beauty and Health Encyclopedia, by Christine Probert (Octopus Books), will provide more information on pampering and health-cum-beauty treatments.

Appendix 13

Some more useful addresses

ACTION ON SMOKING AND HEALTH,
5–11 Mortimer Street,
London, W1N 7RH   Tel. 01–637 9843

BRITISH AND EUROPEAN OSTEOPATHIC SOCIETY,
Orient House,
42–45 New Bond Street,
London, EC2M 1QY   Tel. 01–642 4161

BRITISH HEART FOUNDATION,
102 Gloucester Place,
London, W1H 4DH   Tel. 01–935 0185

THE BRITISH NUTRITION FOUNDATION,
15 Belgrave Square,
London, SW1X 8PS   Tel. 01–235 4904

BRITISH PREGNANCY ADVISORY SERVICE,
Austy Manor,
Wooton Manor,
Solihull,
West Midlands, B95 6BX   Tel. 05642–4225

CORONARY PREVENTION GROUP,
60 Gt Ormond Street,
London, WC1N 3HR   Tel. 01–833 3687

DEPRESSIVES ANONYMOUS,
Self-Help Centre,
83 Derby Road,
Nottingham   Tel. 0602–691212

THE LONDON SCHOOL OF AROMATHERAPY,
PO Box 780,
London, NW6

MENTAL HEALTH FOUNDATION,
10 Hallam Street,
London, W1N 6DH   Tel. 01–580 0145

MILLBANK FILMS LIMITED,
1 Adam Street,
London, WC2N 6AA   Tel. 01–839 7176

SCOTTISH HEALTH EDUCATION GROUP,
Health Education Centre,
Canaan Lane,
Edinburgh, EH10 4SG   Tel. 031–447 8044

SCOTTISH SPORTS COUNCIL,
1 St Colme Street,
Edinburgh, EH3 6AA   Tel. 031–225 8411

SPORTS COUNCIL (ENGLAND),
70 Brompton Road,
London, SW3 1EX   Tel. 01–589 3411

SPORTS COUNCIL FOR NORTHERN IRELAND,
49 Malone Road,
Belfast, BT9 6RZ   Tel. 0232–663 154

SPORTS COUNCIL FOR WALES,
National Sport Centre,
Sophia Gardens,
Cardiff, CF1 9SW   Tel. 0222–397 571

A glossary of terms

Adrenaline A hormone which speeds up the pulse rate and increases blood pressure, stimulates the flow of blood to the brain and other parts of the system and prepares the brain and body for action. Adrenaline is one of the 'stress hormones'.

Atheroma A fatty deposit containing cholesterol which builds up in the lining of the arteries. Serious build-up of atheroma can block the arteries, causing heart attacks and strokes.

Blood pressure The pressure required to push blood through the arteries and the smaller blood vessels.

Calorie A unit of energy. One calorie is defined as the energy needed to raise the temperature of 1 kilogramme of water by 1 degree Celsius. The human body needs about 60 calories an hour to meet the body's normal energy needs.

Cardiac Concerning the heart.

Cholesterol A fatty substance used by the body as a 'building block' for tissues and also for certain chemical processes.

Coronary thrombosis A condition in which one of the coronary arteries surrounding the heart is blocked by a blood clot – also referred to as a 'heart attack'.

Hypertension Seriously high blood pressure. Hypertension can lead to heart disease or a stroke.

Obesity   A condition in which the sufferer is at least 20 per cent above the 'ideal' weight for his or her height.

Stamina   A form of physical fitness giving a person 'staying power', i.e. the ability to sustain physical exercise without becoming markedly breathless. Stamina fitness is thought to help prevent heart attacks.

Stress   An everyday term that covers a number of psychological pressures which can lead to physical ill-health or mental breakdown.

Stroke   Paralysis or other malfunctions due to a sudden lack of blood caused by a clot in a blood vessel (thrombosis) or the rupture of a blood vessel.

Index

Index

Also by Matthew Archer

Call Yourself a Manager!

THROUGHOUT THE business world there are thousands of
people trying desperately hard to become 'a manager'.
Some of those who have made it to a management position
have aspirations of becoming the 'chief executive'. It is not
too difficult to acquire the technical knowledge that goes
with the job but the human element is much more elusive:
managers, being human, are subject to their own
weaknesses and their performance can be affected by their
fears, prejudices, lifestyle and relationships with others.

In this book, based on long experience (the examples are
real – if disguised), the author analyses a wide range of
management styles. In an amusing and readable manner,
the author gives busy managers useful and practical advice
on how to improve their performance and how to make
both their own working lives and those of their staff more
enjoyable and productive.

Published by Mercury Books, W.H. Allen & Co. Plc.